To Ryan,
Best to you
on your leadership
journey!

Fondly,
Joanne
11/25/13

The
HCAHPS
Handbook

Hardwire Your Hospital for
Pay-for-Performance Success

By
Quint Studer
Brian C. Robinson & Karen Cook, RN

Published by:
Fire Starter Publishing
913 Gulf Breeze Parkway, Suite 6
Gulf Breeze, FL 32561
Phone: 850-934-1099
Fax: 850-934-1384
www.firestarterpublishing.com

ISBN: 978-0-9828503-0-5

Library of Congress Control Number: 2010937060

Printed in the United States of America

A Word from the Coauthors

Look at the cover of *The HCAHPS Handbook* and you'll see it's coauthored by Quint Studer, Brian C. Robinson, and Karen Cook, RN. While it's true that the three of us put the book together (along with an army of contributors, editors, and other helpful souls), many others deserve to share the credit.

We want to make it clear that we are only the distillers and reporters of the content in this book. The hard work—the *real* work—was done by two groups that have our eternal gratitude: a) the Studer Group coaches and experts who discovered, harvested, and shared the tactics laid out in this book, and b) the partner organizations that provided the fertile field for the tactics to take root and grow.

The men and women collectively known as Studer Group have spent years doing intensive research in our national learning lab of 700-plus healthcare organizations. They are masters at discovering what the people inside our partner organizations are doing right—and taking that message to others in the field.

The knowledge our coaches refine and share has evolved over time. The tactics they've harvested and refined are a true work in progress and the result of many years of institutional memory. The tactics in this book will continue to evolve as health reform and other changes in the external environment place ever-increasing demands on healthcare organizations.

As for Studer Group partners, we believe they are the finest healthcare professionals in the world. It is their dedication, their passion for helping others, and their generosity of spirit that made this book possible. Every day, they work tirelessly to provide better and better care to the patients they serve.

To both these groups we offer our sincerest thanks. The relationship between our coaches and partners is a symbiotic one. Both parties are enriched by the work of the other—and the real beneficiaries are the patients. May we continue to care for them for many years to come.

Quint Studer
Brian C. Robinson
Karen Cook, RN

This book is dedicated to Cam Underhill. Cam was a true fire starter in each and every way. She spent her life, which ended way too early due to breast cancer, creating what this book is all about: a way to take better care of patients and their families. Cam also understood that to deliver excellent care, it is vital that healthcare providers have the right environment in which to work. This means making sure people have the right development, tools, and techniques so they can provide the care they are committed to.

Cam's flame burns in each of us in the form of an unselfish dedication to serve others.

TABLE OF CONTENTS

INTRODUCTION

Studer Group® partners outperform peers by an average of 20 percentile points across HCAHPS measures. They also outpace them in improvements at a speed nearly three times faster than the nation. And they perform better than the nation in all core measures.

We've been closely studying the Hospital Consumer Assessment of Healthcare Providers and Systems since the very beginning—in fact, even before HCAHPS became the official name. We knew that HCAHPS was going to be far more than the "patient satisfaction surveys" that were being used and would take on ever-greater importance as transparency was expanded and health reform got underway. Studer Group has never been a "patient satisfaction" company. We've always been focused on delivering quality, patient-centered care—hence our understanding that HCAHPS is a metric that represents the patient's perception of *quality* care.

Healthcare organizations realized HCAHPS was important, too. Leaders said things like, "Okay, we're doing great in the Nurse Communication composite. But our Pain Management results are well below national average. We need to perform well on all areas that are important to the patient perception of quality care."

This prompted us to turn to our national learning lab—made up of hundreds and hundreds of top healthcare organizations we work with across the country—and isolate the "best practices" that were helping create and sustain consistently high HCAHPS results for each composite.

We talked with some of the smartest people working in healthcare today, experts known for their laser focus on finding the most effective, efficient ways to do things. (These people are passionate "fire starters" for perfecting techniques and making healthcare better.)

In many cases the tactics we were already helping our clients hardwire naturally aligned with HCAHPS. We simply had to make some minor adaptations to the work they were already doing. Then, everything was processed and boiled down to the most critical points and compiled into one resource: *The HCAHPS Handbook*.

This book does *not* contain an exhaustive list of every tactic Studer Group teaches. Instead, it zeroes in on each HCAHPS question and describes the top two or three tactics proven to make *always* responses more likely—consistently across your organization and over time.

When you get into the composites, you'll find that there are typically several tactics included for each question. We recommend that you pick one tactic and get it to the point to where it's always performed. This allows you to know how aggressive you need to be in implementing the other tactics—or whether you need to use the other tactics at all.

Our research shows that one of the reasons execution fails is because organizations try to implement too much behavioral change at once. What we try to do is focus in on the most specific tactics that will create the most impact for the right reason: to improve patient care.

While *The HCAHPS Handbook* is focused on improving patient care outcomes as measured by HCAHPS, it is our hope that you will keep in mind the *why*. We don't want to encourage "teaching to the test" syndrome. Rather, we encourage leaders and staff members alike to realize that the results are meaningful—that they really do translate to better, more consistent quality care, which in turn translates to better patient outcomes. HCAHPS results are just another way to measure how often we do something that is important to patients—in other words, how often we demonstrate a culture of *always* and provide the very best care.

We know that creating this kind of culture is hard. Many things in healthcare are hard—supply chain management, creating new clinical programs, physician recruiting—but there is probably nothing harder than getting to *always*. It means we need every single person to get it right every single time. That would be difficult in any industry.

But just because something is difficult doesn't mean it's not worthwhile. That's especially true in healthcare. We know that there is no other industry that has such a profound impact on people's lives. And while there is no easy way to create a culture of *always*, we're helping remove the guesswork by providing our partners with Evidence-Based Leadership^{SM} (EBL) tactics that are proven to work. (EBL is our leadership framework. It's designed to reduce variances in leadership skills and processes and help organizations achieve predictable, positive outcomes.)

We hope you find this book helpful—and that it's the first step on a pathway that leads to higher HCAHPS results, better patient outcomes, and a more successful organization.

CHAPTER ONE:

HCAHPS COUNTS: WHY IT'S YOUR KEY TO PAY-FOR-PERFORMANCE SUCCESS

A Brief Introduction to HCAHPS

If you're a newer leader, you may appreciate this quick overview.

HCAHPS stands for "Hospital Consumer Assessment of Healthcare Providers and Systems." Essentially, it's the first national, standardized, publically reported survey of patients' perspectives of hospital care. It was developed by the Centers for Medicare & Medicaid Services (CMS) together with the Agency for Healthcare Research and Quality (AHRQ), another agency in the Department of Health and Human Services.

In May 2005 the National Quality Forum endorsed HCAHPS. Then, in December 2005, the Federal Office of Management and Budget gave its final approval for the survey to be implemented nationally.

In 2006, voluntary collection of HCAHPS data began, and the first public reporting occurred in March

2008. The results were posted on the Hospital Compare website: www.hospitalcompare.hhs.gov.

According to CMS, the survey was shaped by three overarching goals:

1. To produce comparable data on patients' perspectives of care so that consumers can make objective and meaningful comparisons among hospitals

2. To create incentives for hospitals to improve their quality of care

3. To enhance public accountability in healthcare by increasing the transparency of the quality of hospital care

("HCAHPS: Patients' Perspectives of Care Survey." *Centers for Medicare &Medicaid Services. U.S. Department of Health & Human Services.* 21 April 2010. <http://www.cms. gov/HospitalQualityInits/30_HospitalHCAHPS.asp> (27 July 2010).)

HCAHPS is part of a broader value-based purchasing initiative that ties reimbursement to quality outcomes. It is expected to expand to encompass outpatient areas over the next two years.

Before we get into the details, let's first look at HCAHPS in a broader context:

When the Patient Protection and Affordable Care Act was signed into law (March 2010), patient-centered care—quality care—moved from being a legislative and reimbursement issue to being front and center nationwide. The program creates a new urgency for hardwiring high performance. The value-based purchasing (VBP) initiative that begins in FY 2013 will focus on HCAHPS and core measures results.

VBP will transition providers from HCAHPS pay-for-reporting to pay-for-performance, and the amount of reimbursement tied to the survey will potentially double by 2017. It's clearly about how well your organization can demonstrate that it has hardwired quality.

The following graphic illustrates how the VBP initiative will determine hospital reimbursement:

Figure 1.1

CMS Value-Based Purchasing

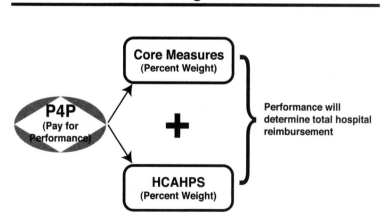

Implementation FY 2013 (Oct. 2012)

Also beginning in 2013: CMS will impose financial penalties on what it deems "excess admissions" compared to expected levels for 30-day readmissions of patients with specific diagnoses. The legislation also asks hospitals to collaborate with physicians to provide leadership in accountable care organizations (ACOs), which create shared responsibility for meeting certain quality and cost savings targets.

Pay-for-quality is here to stay. If ever there was a time to hardwire a culture of excellent patient care—to ensure your organization is consistently meeting its mission, protecting its bottom line, and enhancing its reputation—that time has clearly arrived. The good news: If you've hardwired Studer Group's Evidence-Based Leadership^{SM} framework and tools, you will be well-positioned in the future operating environment.

Understanding the Basics

HCAHPS provides consumers with information that is helpful in choosing a hospital and standardizes questions for public comparisons.

Hospitals must submit a minimum of 300 surveys of eligible patients (18 years or older discharged from general acute care hospitals after an overnight stay) for each reporting period. Along with core measures and other quality metrics, the patients' perception of their experience results can be viewed at www.hospitalcompare.hhs. gov.

The site is very user-friendly. Go ahead and check the results of your hospital and two competitors. How does your organization measure up?

The survey questions measure frequency (rather than satisfaction) on six composites (or categories) of questions and two additional questions. The scale is *never, sometimes, usually,* or *always* with regard to:

- Communication with doctors
- Communication with nurses
- Responsiveness of hospital staff
- Pain management
- Communication about medications
- Cleanliness of hospital
- Quietness at night of hospital

There is one more composite and three additional questions whose answers are in other formats:

- Discharge information—no to yes
- Willingness to recommend—definitely no to definitely yes
- Overall hospital rating—0 to 10 rating scale

The percentage of patients who give their hospital a rating overall of 9 or 10 are reported as the top-box result (on a scale from 0 to 10), as well as the percent of patients who report definitely yes, they would be willing to recommend the hospital.

The "top box"—or most frequently reported *best* result in each composite—is reported for each hospital. In other words, if 75 percent of your surveyed patients reported that their nurses "always" communicated well, 20 percent said they "sometimes" communicated well, and 5 percent said they "never" communicated well, 75 percent is reported in response to that question. It's important to note that only *always* counts. There is no partial credit for "almost" (like patient satisfaction vendors provide).

Ask your vendors to provide percentage breakdowns of patient responses by unit. This will help you determine opportunities for improvement. It's important to focus first on units that are performing at mid-level. Just as it's easier to move a B to an A than a C to an A, it's easier to move a *usually* to an *always* than to move a *never* to an *always*.

Figure 1.2

HCAHPS "Top-Box Percentiles" Public Reporting

HCAHPS "TOP-BOX PERCENTILES" - December 2009 Public Reporting*

Percentile among reporting hospitals**	Communication with Nurses	Communication with Doctors	Responsiveness of Hosp. Staff	Pain Management	Comm. about Medicines	Cleanliness of Hospital Env.	Quietness of Hospital Env.	Discharge Information	Overall Hospital Rating	Recommend the Hospital
5th	62	70	47	58	48	56	40	71	48	50
25th	70	76	56	65	55	64	48	77	59	61
50th	75	80	62	68	58	69	55	81	65	68
75th	79	83	69	72	63	75	63	84	71	75
95th	85	89	79	78	71	84	76	88	81	85

* Percentiles for HCAHPS "top-box" scores of 3,766 hospitals publicly reported in December 2009 on *Hospital Compare*. Survey results are from patients discharged between April 2008 and March 2009. Scores have been adjusted for survey mode and patient-mix.

** For example, 5% of hospitals scored 62 or lower (5th percentile) on the "Communication with Nurses" measure, and 5% scored 85 or higher (95th percentile). The median score (50th percentile) on this measure was 75.

http://www.hcahpsonline.org/Executive_Insight/Files/HCAHPS%20Percentiles%2012-17-2009.pdf

Using the database of 3,766 hospitals that report their data, it is relatively easy to determine the organization's performance as compared to all others. While the CMS website doesn't officially rank hospitals yet, this is relatively easy to do.

Important Things to Consider:

1. There is a clear connection between quality and patient satisfaction. HCAHPS has elevated our attention to delivering patient-centered care. Historically, some have considered patient satisfaction "soft" or a "nice to have." Never has this been *less* true than it is today. The patient's perception of his or her care is a tangible reflection of your delivery of quality care.

That's just one of the reasons that Studer Group's Individualized Patient Care (IPC) tactic—an approach to care that incorporates the patient's thoughts on what very good or excellent care means to him or her—has driven high patient satisfaction so reliably over recent years in hospitals nationwide. Also, the HCAHPS frequency scale measures how often certain events occur and reports it with other clinical quality measures. *Always* means that every interaction occurs with every patient on every shift!

Many HCAHPS questions offer feedback on issues that impact core clinical quality, such as communicating medication side effects, managing pain well, and explaining discharge instructions in a way patients can understand. In fact, patients and their families are the only source of information about many aspects of quality. By involving them in the redesign of care and quality improvement, we improve our opportunity for quality, efficiency, better clinical outcomes, and reimbursement maximization.

2. **It may seem that nurses are the heart and soul of HCAHPS success—but don't ignore the impact of other staff members.** Nurse communication is highly correlated with patients' overall hospital rating. And it's true that if your HCAHPS overall results are low, you should review your organization's performance on this composite (how often were patients treated with respect, how often did nurses listen carefully, and how often did nurses explain things in ways patients could understand).

However, it's also true that patients tend to perceive everyone they come in contact with as either "a doctor" or "a nurse"—even if they're really from an ancillary or support department. They just don't make the distinction. So while nursing-sensitive indicators are driving the HCAHPS results, the overall perception of care is impacted by every interaction the patient has with a staff member.

That is why goal alignment is so important to success of HCAHPS. When ancillary partners carry goals for areas they own or share goals with nursing, it creates true synergy. Everyone works toward the same outcomes.

3. **A consistent culture of excellence is vital.** Patients expect a basic level of service and quality when entering your hospital. Your organization

can sustain excellence at exceeding patient expectations only if you have an engaged, satisfied, and high-performing team of physicians, caregivers, and support staff.

Ask yourself: Do you consistently retain high performers and show no tolerance for low performers? Do employees believe leaders "walk the talk" with respect to mission, vision, and values? Do you identify and address any barriers to culture change and quality of work life for employees to improve your HCAHPS patient perception of care?

The HCAHPS frequency scale demands that you demonstrate zero tolerance for employees who are rude or violate your organization's behavior standards. The days of tolerating a staff member with good clinical skills who is otherwise abrupt or even rude with patients are over.

Rethinking HCAHPS: Your Compass for Navigating an Uncertain Future

In healthcare, our real goal is always to provide better patient care. However, dollars are a lifeline for hospitals. That's just reality. Adequate revenues are needed to provide care and to invest in new technologies and equipment as well as new facilities. Revenue impacts the future of an organization and impacts its ability to add services and improve access.

So how *do* we maximize our reimbursement opportunities and find the resources to meet the healthcare needs of our communities? Focusing on HCAHPS is one answer.

When HCAHPS was first announced, many people thought, *Oh, another patient satisfaction survey...and a government one at that.* Maybe you did, too. But there is a big difference. Perhaps the most obvious one is that traditional patient satisfaction results can be kept private. HCAHPS results cannot. Organizations can no longer control the flow of information regarding how their patients perceive their care (indeed, competitors can easily release your scores). The survey truly heralds a new age of transparency.

Plus, as we've already said (and will continue to say), HCAHPS goes much deeper than "satisfaction." So now, in light of healthcare reform, it's time to take another look at this survey and its relevance. It is time to look at the evidence and see how we can use it to improve our organizations.

HCAHPS Results and Clinical Outcomes Are Two Sides of the Same Coin

The *New England Journal of Medicine* found that quality of care was significantly better in hospitals that performed better on HCAHPS. The data also supports that the patient's experience is linked to great clinical care, reduced medical error, and advanced performance outcomes.

At Studer Group® our findings directly tie to those of the *New England Journal of Medicine*. As we worked with our partners to improve clinical outcomes, we observed their corresponding HCAHPS results went up, too. We now know many of these clinical outcomes were tied to the same metrics as future health reform reimbursement.

Here's the point: HCAHPS results go hand-in-hand with clinical quality metrics. So when we improve those results, we also improve our clinical care. And because the metrics that determine both are the metrics by which we'll be judged and compensated in the future, we also improve our likelihood of maximizing our reimbursement.

We can create cultures of consistent excellence. We can become more efficient, more effective, and more transparent in order to not only deliver on our mission but also to meet the standards the government is going to hold us to in the future. We *can* get it right—not sometimes, but all the time—every day in every department with every patient. Every patient who comes to us for their healthcare needs deserves no less.

Why HCAHPS Is a Catalyst for Quality

HCAHPS results are a natural metric for determining what kind of job we're doing in caring for our patients—and pinpointing where we need improvement.

"Patient perception of care" is a whole lot more than making sure nurses and doctors are friendly and smiling. It's about saving lives and delivering safe healthcare. It's about quality in a very real, concrete way. It's about using HCAHPS results as a metric, a barometer for measuring clinical performance and improvement.

HCAHPS gives us a way to drill down into the details and discover what processes will positively and consistently impact the patient perception of quality but also better patient clinical outcomes: fewer falls, lower infection rates, fewer bed sores, fewer readmissions, and so forth. It gives us a national benchmark by which to measure the quality we're seeking to achieve.

Yes, We *Can* Improve Quality

The best news is we know exactly how to achieve better outcomes. We know, right now, which tools and techniques make them happen. Why? Because we have research, conducted via our national learning lab of hundreds of top hospitals, that clearly demonstrates what works.

When we talk to hospitals that consistently score high in the responsiveness and pain management composites, we usually hear about hardwired Hourly Rounding[SM]. By checking on the patient every hour and communicating regarding pain and personal needs, you raise patients' perception of care. This translates to improved HCAHPS results and corresponding improvements in clinical outcomes.

The *American Journal of Nursing* reported on the effectiveness of Studer Group tactics, showing that Hourly Rounding leads to decreased falls by 50 percent and skin breakdown by 14 percent. As our partners implement Studer Group's evidence-based tools and techniques, they also see a correlating improvement in hospital-acquired conditions. And their reportable quality metrics go up as well. (Our partners outperform the nation on all core measures.) These improvements, as well as their improvement in HCAHPS results, position hospitals to be better prepared for reform changes coming in the future.

Studer Group coaches tell their partners that if they are using the tools we recommend and are still not seeing improvement in clinical metrics and corresponding HCAHPS improvements, it's time for them to dig deeper. It's time to make sure they are doing it effectively instead of just doing it. It is about quality of initiatives and not quantity. This thinking aligns with the platform of this book.

Research has shown that proper use of these strategies will deliver big returns. Quality improvements will generate efficiencies that save money.

Consistency Is Everything

Here's the reality. Many hospitals that focus a great deal of attention on something will see moderate improvements—unfortunately, they then shift their focus, and the results drop. We see this with key initiatives like Hourly Rounding. An organization will "roll out" Hourly Rounding, everyone will get trained, and leaders will focus heavily on the initiative. They will see jumps in their scores or sudden surges of improvement (which regress the next year). Some units may start to get great HCAHPS results while others lag behind.

Such instances of sporadic, partial, or temporary improvement aren't that difficult to achieve. But they also aren't good enough. To fulfill the mission and maximize for pay-for-performance-related reimbursement, you need to deliver high-quality, efficient, and responsive care *consistently.*

Long-term, sustainable gains are much more difficult to achieve. It also could be said that if you are not getting better, you are getting worse—because every hospital in the country is focusing on this subject.

Organizations must put an infrastructure in place that allows them to quickly improve their HCAHPS results and consistently meet the high standards by which we will be judged and compensated in the future.

The infrastructure proven to generate this level of efficiency and effectiveness? Evidence-Based Leadership. As you'll recall, Studer Group partners (who use EBL as a framework) outperform the nation on HCAHPS, outpace it in improvements, and also beat the national average in every core measure.

EBL: A System for Creating an Aligned, Accountable Infrastructure

What is Evidence-Based Leadership (EBL)? It's a framework that allows organizations to create a system of aligned goals and absolute accountability that ensures people will execute well every time. EBL provides a foundation that allows organizations to quickly drill down to the tactics that most impact their desired outcomes. This framework ensures leaders have the skills to execute in a nimble and consistent manner.

As healthcare delivery is impacted by reform, organizations that have embraced the EBL framework are able to incorporate or emphasize tactics proven to get results.

As different sections of the Patient Protection and Affordable Care Act are implemented, EBL becomes increasingly critical. It provides the foundation that allows our partners to respond faster and more effectively to industry changes.

Figure 1.3

Execution Framework
Evidence-Based Leadership

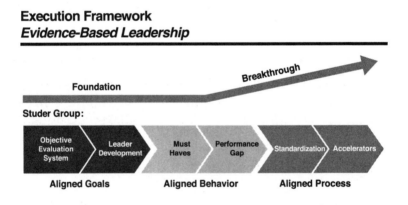

Arming Yourself to Maximize Quality and Reimbursement

The intrinsic motivation to provide improved care resonates with most healthcare workers. That said, there is also validity to the old adage "no margin, no mission." And now, as we think about not only HCAHPS but future changes associated with the Patient Protection and Affordable Care Act, it's clear that reimbursement will become an even greater focus as sections of the law are implemented.

Of course, while HCAHPS and core measures are the first programmatic aspect of health reform to be rolled out, they are only a small part of the picture. Many other aspects of the law, including hospital-acquired conditions, preventable readmissions, and accountable care organizations, will eventually be linked to reimbursement.

What's more, private health insurance companies have already begun to follow the government's lead. Regardless of where it's coming from, reimbursement will be increasingly tied to performance on quality initiatives.

The good news is that the clinical processes we focus on to improve HCAHPS results are also related to most of the issues on which reimbursement will be based. When you get HCAHPS improvement tactics hardwired into your organization—coupled with an EBL framework that holds people accountable for using them—you've already won half the battle.

The bottom line is that with all the changes coming—and with all the implications from the Patient Protection and Affordable Care Act—excellent quality, increased efficiency and effectiveness, and extraordinary responsiveness are prerequisites for survival.

What you must do now is put an infrastructure in place that enables you to quickly and consistently achieve and maintain higher and higher levels of quality and efficiency. It's the only way to set yourself up for success in a future where nothing is certain—except for change.

Don't Forget the ED: Why a Patient's "First Impression" Sets the Stage for HCAHPS Success

You might find it odd that we would zero-in on the Emergency Department in a book about an inpatient survey. But when you think about how your patients get to your hospital in the first place, it makes perfect sense.

The Emergency Department is the major point of entry for the largest number of patients arriving at your hospital. Nationally, the ED accounts for 50 percent of inpatient admissions, 75 percent of plain radiographs, and 50 percent of CT scans and ultrasounds in the entire hospital.

First the bad news: Research performed during the HCAHPS testing period found that patients admitted through the Emergency Department rated care across all composites more negatively than those patients admitted through other avenues. Vendors that administer inpatient perception of care surveys have found that admission through the ED also negatively affects IP results.

The implication is clear. When a patient has a poor perception of the care he received in your Emergency Department, it's almost impossible to recover from it. That's why it's so critical to make a good "first impression"—to set the stage for a successful stay and, by extension, favorable HCAHPS results.

Studer Group's own research shows that as ED perception of care results improve, so do inpatient results. Our partner data also indicates that by improving ED patient perception of care results, hospitals can also expect to see higher HCAHPS results in all ten composites. The data below shows the relationship between ED percentile rank and HCAHPS "overall" percentile rank.

We looked at the 180 hospitals for which Studer Group has both ED perception of care results and HCAHPS results for patients discharged during the period October 2008-September 2009. We found a statistically significant correlation between ED percentile ranking and HCAHPS percentile ranking for the "Patients who rated the hospital a 9 or 10" question (r=.486), meaning that as one goes up so does the other, and the likelihood that this occurs by chance is less than 1 percent.

We categorized each of the hospitals by their year average ED percentile rank, as shown in the table below, and then looked within each category at the hospital's HCAHPS "percent 9s and 10s" average percentile rank.

The chart on the following page shows that as a hospital's ED percentile ranking increases, so does the HCAHPS "percent 9s and 10s" percentile ranking.

Figure 1.4

Relationship between Emergency Department Percentile Rank and HCAHPS "Overall" Percentile Rank

HCAHPS "TOP-BOX PERCENTILES" - Patients Discharged from October 2008 to September 2009

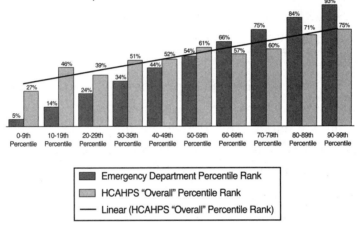

Percentiles for HCAHPS were publicly reported on the *Hospital Compare* Website.
Emergency Department percentile rankings are from Studer Group internal measurement documents.

Organizations focused on improving their HCAHPS results would do well to focus on ensuring that ED patients have the best possible experience.

Now the good news: EBL tactics designed for the in-patient environment are easily modified for the ED setting to drive consistency of the patient experience.

Studer Group has various resources devoted solely to this subject—among them the Fire Starter Publishing books *Excellence in the Emergency Department: How to Get Results* by Stephanie Baker, RN, CEN, MBA, and *Hardwiring Flow: Systems and Processes for Seamless Patient Care* by Thom

Mayer, MD, FACEP, FAAP, and Kirk Jensen, MD, MBA, FACEP.

When you improve your Emergency Department, you improve your entire hospital—and your HCAHPS results, as well as your financial state, can only benefit.

A Desk Reference for Busy Professionals

This isn't the kind of book you read in one sitting. We know you don't have time for that. We designed it be a user-friendly "desk reference" of sorts—a trusted resource you reference to focus on specific opportunities for improvement with targeted strategies.

You just read a section that briefly explains HCAHPS and puts it in context with health reform changes. And you're about to learn about a few foundational tactics you need to know in order to improve your HCAHPS results.

Eight tactical sections, each centered on a different HCAHPS composite or question, make up the heart of this book. Within each section, a separate chapter is devoted to each survey question that falls under that particular composite. Chapters feature detailed descriptions of two or three tactics proven to increase the likelihood of an *always* (*yes* or 10) response to the questions they spotlight.

This layout allows readers to quickly find the HCAHPS question they want to target for improvement. Once they've brought up that particular result, they can move on to the next problem area.

Finally, there's a chapter that helps you validate whether people are executing the tactics effectively and consistently.

Remember, the tactics and tools in this book have been field-tested by Studer Group partners who consistently enjoy HCAHPS results that are higher than those of peer organizations. Consistency is the key in creating a culture of every patient, every time, every interaction. That is hardwired excellence—or a culture of *always*.

Chapter Two:

THE FUNDAMENTALS: WHAT YOU MUST KNOW TO IMPROVE YOUR HCAHPS SCORES

As you read *The HCAHPS Handbook,* you will encounter basic tactics that will increase your likelihood of creating a culture of consistent excellence. You'll notice that certain ones come up again and again. These are the "fundamentals"—evidence-based tactics that have significant impact on multiple HCAHPS composites. Master them and you'll be able to tweak them to impact any composite you're trying to move.

Your entire staff will need to be proficient in these tactics in order to move your HCAHPS results up and—even more important— keep them up. Remember that to create a culture of *always* we must ensure that this proficiency is visible in every employee, every time, and with every interaction. Studer Group has numerous tools and resources that can help you learn about these fundamentals and action steps to hardwire them in your organization. Here is a brief overview of each:

Individualized Patient Care (IPC)

It's well documented that patient-centered care improves outcomes. Studer Group took this concept and operationalized it, not just putting the patient at the center but actually customizing and personalizing his or her care. The only one who can tell us what is truly important to the patient is the patient. That is why we call it Individualized Patient Care (IPC)—because we focus on the individual.

We take the technical aspects of care and link them to the individual patient via standardized communication with him or her. As a result, clinical outcomes and patient perception of care improve. More importantly, this provides a mechanism for our staff to get to know the patient as a person.

Basically, IPC allows us to gather a patient's thoughts on what excellent care means to her and to incorporate it into our interactions with her. It also allows us to use this information to better connect with the patient and to "humanize" our care. It's easy to come across as simply going through the motions when we assess patients—IPC helps alleviate that "robotic" effect. We recommend standardization and consistency in asking relevant questions but we do not recommend scripting.

IPC means frequently reviewing performance on what's most important to a patient throughout her stay. Not only does this boost patient perception of care, it improves communication between the patient and hospital employees and encourages teamwork and efficiency. The only way we can truly deliver care that is important to the patient is to first understand what is important and then ask frequently how well we are doing.

Implement Individualized Patient Care at the time of admission assessment by asking the patient the following types of questions:

- "Our goal is to consistently provide excellent care to you. To do this we need to know what excellent care means to you. Can you please tell us?"
- "We want to do everything we can to help keep your pain manageable. Where are you on a pain scale of 1-10?"
- "Where would you like to be on the pain scale?"
- "Is there anything you would like me to know about you that will help me care for you?"

Write the patient's responses on her whiteboard or an Individualized Patient Care card. This is especially useful with pain management and communication of medication composites. As you'll read later, writing down important information such as when the patient's next pain medication is due makes an impact on her perception of care. As nurses and other staff enter the room, they can see what is important to the patient and customize their interactions based on this information. What's important to the patient should be considered during every interaction.

Figure 2.1

How to Implement Individualized Patient Care

Action	How it works
1. Use key words.	Upon admission, the nurse says to the patient: "Our goal is to provide very good care. (Use appropriate language from your patient satisfaction survey.) What three things can we do to make sure your care is very good?" If the patient doesn't know, dig deeper using items from the survey. Say: "How important is your pain management? Keeping you informed? Ensuring your call lights are answered?"
2. Note items on the whiteboard.	There should be a whiteboard in every patient's room. Also write the patient's pain goal and the next time medication is due.
3. Ask during daily rounds.	The nurse manager should ask, "How well are we doing (with each of identified needs)?" and connect these to survey questions.
4. Ask at shift change.	Nursing staff should repeat as above.
5. Ask at discharge.	Both nursing staff and case managers should ask, "How well have we done at (identified needs)?"
6. Review the survey tool.	At discharge, the case manager should review the survey tool. Say, "We survey our patients. It is one way we learn how we are doing and is a way to recognize staff. Will you please do me a favor and complete and return this when it arrives in the mail? Thank you. This is so important to us." (Note: If the patient is not happy, use service recovery!)
7. Make post-visit phone calls.	During the call, ask how well the hospital did at meeting the needs identified by the patient.

IPC can be utilized in all care areas of the hospital including Inpatient, Outpatient, Ambulatory Surgery, and Emergency Departments. By asking patients to tell you what excellent care means to them, you can avoid or immediately address situations that may create unnecessary anxiety and detract from the healing process.

Key Words at Key Times

We at Studer Group have long recommended the use of Key Words at Key Times—carefully chosen words healthcare professionals use to "connect the dots" and help patients, families, and visitors better understand what we are doing—and most importantly, *why*.

Every day we deal with patients who are distracted, frightened, and many times in pain. We may think we have communicated something, but in reality what we thought we were communicating may not have been heard.

Key words are a simple way to solve that problem. They help the patient understand his/her care better, they reduce anxiety and build trust, and they align the behavior of the staff to the needs of the patient. When we talk about key words, we are really talking about building a relationship with our patients during their most vulnerable time of need.

AIDET^{SM} (also called the Five Fundamentals of Communication) is a good platform for applying key words. More specifically, it's a communication framework that improves patients' perception of their care, helps reduce their anxiety (thus improving outcomes), builds patient loyalty, and ensures that your staff is delivering the same consistent messages of concern and appreciation.

AIDET is an acronym that stands for **A**cknowledge, **I**ntroduce, **D**uration, **E**xplanation, and **T**hank You. When organizations incorporate AIDET into daily practices, the results are amazing.

A Sample AIDET Conversation

A Good morning, Mrs. Smith.

I I am Megan and I'm the radiology technologist who will do your CT scan today. I've been at this hospital for 10 years, and I have done over 2,000 of these tests. You are in very good hands with our team.

D I am going to take about five minutes to explain this to you and then we will do the procedure. You should be ready to go back to your room in about 30 minutes. Shall we get started?

E First, we are going to start an IV. Are you right- or left-handed? Next we will... (explain the steps of the procedure).

T We are all finished. Thank you so much for holding still; we got some very good information for the doctor to review. Is there anything I can do for you before I leave?

Remember, in a culture of *always*, a patient is judging every employee and every interaction. The Radiology Department that standardizes and holds people accountable for using AIDET will impact the overall perception of the patient experience in a very positive way. Courtesy and respect apply to everyone, and this is just one example of how AIDET promotes these values.

It is important to note that all the letters in AIDET do not have to be implemented at once. In fact, with many of the HCAHPS composites, one or two letters are emphasized. For example, if your unit is focusing on Communication of Medications, remind the staff to focus on the "E" for explanation of medication side effects.

Organizations that have leveraged the power of key words are exceptional at answering the following questions: What do our patients want to know? What do we need for our patients to know? How can we help patients/visitors feel comfortable with our care and procedures? Are we communicating clear messages to everyone, every time?

When AIDET is hardwired, you can expect to see improved perception of care by patients and their families. You can even drive "unit loyalty." We've seen patients request a certain unit upon a return visit or ask for a specific care team based on their prior experience.

Hourly Rounding

Studer Group's Hourly Rounding tactic has a tremendous impact on patient perception and quality of care. The September 2006 *American Journal of Nursing* published a study showing evidence that when implemented and hardwired, Hourly Rounding effectively decreases call lights by 37.8 percent; decreases falls by 50 percent; decreases hospital-acquired decubiti by 14 percent; and improves patient perception by 12 mean points.

What *is* Hourly Rounding? Simply put, it's making a commitment to have a staff member visit every patient every one to two hours. This doesn't just mean "checking in," however—it means practicing a series of eight very specific behaviors. Here are the eight behaviors and the composites they address:

1 Use opening key words to reduce anxiety (AIDET). (Nurse Communication)

2. Perform scheduled tasks. (Communication about Medications)

3. Address the "Three Ps"—pain, potty, position. (Responsiveness and Pain Management)

4. Assess additional comfort needs. (Quietness)

5. Conduct environmental assessment. (Cleanliness)

6. Ask, "Is there anything else I can do for you? I have time." (Courtesy and Respect)

7. Tell each patient when you will be back. (Responsiveness)

8. Document the process in a rounding log posted in the patient's room.

Each of these behaviors creates a specific desired outcome. Many times staff and leaders are tempted to "modify" rounds by eliminating certain steps. But in doing so, you're reducing the impact and losing some of the successful outcomes you can achieve.

Figure 2.2

Eight Behaviors for Hourly Rounds

Hourly Rounding Behavior	Expected Results
Use opening key words	Contributes to efficiency
Accomplish scheduled tasks	Contributes to efficiency
Address Three Ps (pain, potty, position)	Quality indicators – falls, decubitis, pain management
Address additional comfort needs	Improved patient satisfaction on pain, concern and caring
Conduct environmental assessment	Contributes to efficiency, teamwork
Ask, "Is there anything else I can do for you before I go? I have time."	Contributes to efficiency; Improves patient satisfaction on teamwork and communication
Tell each patient when you will be back	Contributes to efficiency
Document the round	Quality and accountability

When presenting Hourly Rounding to nurses, focus on quality and safe patient care. Refer them to the call-light statistic mentioned earlier and connect the dots on what is in it for them. That study, performed on data from 27 nursing units in 14 hospitals, revealed that nurses who rounded hourly reduced call lights by 4,901 in a four-week period. If an average response to a call light is estimated to take four minutes, nurses saved 326 hours per month or 81.5 hours each week responding to call lights.

Hourly Rounding gets results. When staff members start seeing these results in their daily work lives, they'll naturally want to become more efficient and effective. When they see that patients are healthier and happier, their enthusiasm will increase even more. Before long, not only will patients be giving higher HCAHPS results, the organization will keep getting better and better.

Tip: Nurse Leader Rounding (also in this section) should be hardwired before Hourly Rounding is implemented to ensure consistency and accountability.

Bedside Shift Report

This initiative refers to the process of handing off care delivery from one nurse to another at change of shift at the patient bedside when appropriate. It incorporates other concepts such as managing up, AIDET communication, teamwork, and creating a safe patient environment. All necessary patient information is exchanged in the patient room, such as patient identifiers, safety checks, medications, tests, and so forth. This keeps patients informed and involved in their care, which is a basic patient right. It is also a nurse satisfier as it promotes teamwork.

This initiative will help hospitals demonstrate compliance with National Patient Safety Goals (NPSGs) regarding handoffs and transitions of care by allowing patients to hear their care plan and ask questions of their caregivers. This can be done in the IP, OP, and ED setting and can be adapted to ANY handoff or transition of care—meaning every time a patient moves from one place to another or from one caregiver to another, the patient is included in his care.

Here is an example:

Good morning, Mr. Jones. I am going home now, and Karen is going to be your nurse today. Karen has been with us for three years. I'm leaving you in very good hands.

I'm going to give her the report now, so that she has all the information she needs to take very good care of you today. Please listen, and when I am through, I'd like you to tell Karen about the new medication you started today. If I've left out anything important for Karen to know, please tell us before we leave.

(Verbally gives report to Karen)

Okay, Mr. Jones, can you tell Karen about the new medication you started today? Tell her why you are taking it and what common side effect we talked about.

Mr. Jones, do you have questions for me before I leave? Is there anything more that Karen needs to know in order to provide you with excellent care today?

I'm heading home now. Thank you for allowing me to be part of your care team last night.

Here are a few of the benefits of Bedside Reporting:

Figure 2.3

Handoffs and Bedside Report-
Benefits

- Decreases potential for misses and mistakes.
- Increases patient involvement and addresses keeping patients informed.
- Increases trust for patient with managing up.
- Decreases patient waiting at change of shift and feeling forgotten or abandoned.
- Increases accountability for nurses as they report off visually in front of the patient and each other.
- Increases new RN skill level—RNs can see and hear what the experienced RN is doing and why.
- Increases teamwork between shifts.

This tactic saves lives by ensuring safe handoffs. It also keeps patients informed about their care and reduces their anxiety by "managing up" the care provider and decreasing the perception that "nobody is around at shift change." It is a real-time exchange of information that increases patient safety (sentinel events also occur more often during this time), improves quality of care, increases accountability, and strengthens teamwork.

Nurse Leader Rounding

Nurse leader rounding is a *proactive* plan to engage, listen to, communicate with, build relationships with, and support the most important patients and their families. This tactic is a structured mechanism to ensure that quality, safe, and compassionate care is delivered to every patient, every time.

Leaders ask targeted questions to obtain *actionable* information. They can use this information to coach or reward and recognize staff in real-time fashion. When hardwired, this tactic will drive better patient outcomes and results, as well as differentiate your organization from your competitors.

The goal of rounding is that nurse leaders—or their properly trained delegates—will round on every patient every day. This is when you will see the biggest and most sustained impact. If this is not possible, patients should be rounded on at least once during their stay. It allows nurse leaders to connect with patients to reinforce care, verify nursing behaviors, and recognize staff members who go above and beyond the call of duty.

Nurse leaders can use questions strategically. In other words, they can design the questions they ask patients around the initiatives they're focusing on to improve care—managing pain, for instance.

After rounding has been completed, they ask themselves:

1. What have I learned about the care of my patients?

2. What must I do with this information?

If the leader learns that care is being delivered at the highest level, she can immediately reward the behaviors she was verifying. Alternately, she can take the opportunity to coach the staff on how to improve the care provided. Think of leader rounds on patients as a catalyst for making lasting changes that will improve the care of all patients.

This tactic is not easy to implement. At first, it will unearth process improvement opportunities and require nurse leaders to spend additional time rewarding and recognizing and dealing with subpar performers. In other words, it creates more work upfront.

And it will take some time, especially on lower performing units where there are multiple complaints. Again, this is exactly *why* nurse leaders should be rounding on every patient. If patients are complaining in the hospital, they certainly are not going to stop when they go home, and they are going to tell all their friends. This is an excellent opportunity for service recovery!

But once your nurse leaders have been at it for a while—after processes have been improved, systems are working well, and low performers have been moved up or out—they'll find it one of the most enjoyable parts of their jobs. Why? Because it allows them to reconnect with patients, which is probably why they went into nursing in the first place. And they will hear about the excellent care the nurses are providing…and sharing these compliments from the patients is one of the best parts of this challenging job.

Post-Visit Patient Phone Calls

This refers to a process for the staff to connect with patients following discharge to confirm compliance and understanding of discharge instructions, demonstrate empathy, and afford an opportunity for service recovery if appropriate. Outcomes of hardwiring post-visit calls include:

- Reduced patient anxiety
- Increased compliance with discharge instructions
- Improved clinical outcomes
- Reduced readmissions
- Decreased complaints and claims
- Increased employee satisfaction
- Increased patient perception of care

Studer Group recommends that all organizations get a system in place for making post-visit calls—they should become a part of your culture and an extension of your care.

There is much data that supports the need for aggressive use of post-visit patient calls. For instance:

- According to the Agency for Healthcare Research and Quality (AHRQ), heart failure (HF) represents $25 to $35 billion of healthcare expenditures each year; readmissions have tripled in the past 25 years and are expected to triple again over the next 30 years.

- According to AHRQ, the high rate of re-hospitalization for HF patients results from patients' inability to adequately self-manage the condition:
  - ○ National average readmission rate 30 days post-discharge ranges from 18 to 20 percent depending on the region of the country.
  - ○ Thirteen percent of these readmissions were "potentially avoidable," based on the IPPS rule, with major areas of concern including poor communication with patients at discharge, especially around medications, and inadequate post-discharge monitoring.
  - ○ Prevention of these avoidable readmissions could save Medicare $12 billion per year. ("CMS Targets Readmission Through Payment, Audits; 'Coaching' Model Reduces Rates." Report on Medicare Compliance 17, no. 24 (2008): 1-2.)

- Using interactive care, such as post-visit calls, organizations have been able to achieve a 74 percent reduction in HF readmission rate 30 days post-discharge, resulting in an overall readmission rate of 5 percent.

- At the same time, the organizations saw a 43 percent improvement in patient satisfaction.

Since we know that most adverse events will occur within 72 hours of discharge, Studer Group recommends that these calls be made prior to that timeframe. While it is ideal for a clinical staff member to call the patient, any call is better than no call.

It is valuable for staff to hear how the patients perceive their care. Ideally, calls take place within a 24-72-hour timeframe (or until the nurse has made three attempts).

Besides the fact that post-visit calls reduce readmissions, improve clinical outcomes, and save lives, they also reinforce a patient's perception of having received the very best care. And last but not least, they also offer staff members the chance to hear firsthand what a difference they make in the lives of their patients.

Figure 2.4

Post-Visit Phone Call Sample

Empathy and Concern	*"Mrs. Smith? Hello. This is <name>. You were discharged from my unit yesterday. I just wanted to call and see how you're doing today."*
Clinical Outcomes	• *"Do you have any questions regarding your medications or any possible side effects?"* • *"Is your pain well controlled?"* • *"We want to make sure we do excellent clinical follow-up to ensure your best possible recovery. Do you know what symptoms or health problems to look out for?"* • *"Do you have your follow-up appointment?"*
Reward and Recognition	• *"Mrs. Smith, we like to recognize our employees. Who did an excellent job for you while you were in the hospital?"* • *"Can you tell me why Sue was excellent?"*
Service	*"We want to make sure you were very satisfied with your care. How were we, Mrs. Smith?"*
Process Improvement	*"We're always looking to get better. Do you have any suggestions for what we could do to be even better?"*
Appreciation	*"We appreciate your taking the time this afternoon to speak with us about your follow-up care. Is there anything I can do for you?"*

Section One:

Nursing Communication

W hat makes this composite so critical? For starters, HCAHPS correlation data indicates this is the composite most highly correlated with overall hospital rating.

In the patient's mind, most hospital staff members fall into two groups: doctor or nurse. If a patient is wheeled down to radiology and sees someone in scrubs, he or she perceives this person as a nurse. In other words, all staff members have potential to impact this composite's re-sults—so all staff members should be trained in the tac-tics revealed in this section of *The HCAHPS Handbook*.

Studer Group® coaches its partners to train all staff members who interact with patients in these and other tactics. It's working. Our partners outperform the rest of the industry in this composite by nearly 20 percentile points.

Before we delve into the HCAHPS questions that en-compass nurse communication, we'd like to share a story that shows how these tactics affect patients on a personal level—including impacting their clinical outcome:

Mr. Kelly was an elderly patient on the medical/surgical unit. He suffered from a cardiac disorder. During the Bedside Shift Report^{SM}, the exiting nurse reviewed medications with Mr. Kelly and the oncoming nurse. During this conversation, Mr. Kelly asked about his water pill. Upon review, we found that the water pill (Lasix) was not listed on his chart.

We were able to speak to Mr. Kelly's doctor and confirm that, indeed, he needed Lasix added to his medications. Fluid balance is very important for a patient with a cardiac disorder. Had we not included Mr. Kelly in this conversation, his care would certainly have been impacted in a negative way.
- Alejandra, Nurse

It's true that there are many technical aspects to being a great nurse. However, if we focus only on our technical abilities, we can miss things. In Alejandra's story above, had the oncoming nurse just read the medications on the chart or even gone over them with the departing nurse, she may not have noticed a critical medication was missing.

It's important to note upfront that we are asking nurses to provide "more words, not more work." Generally, it's a matter of explaining what we're doing as we're doing it. This eases the patient's anxiety and provides a valuable "win" for the nurse.

The more we interact with patients, the more we learn about them and the stronger the relationships are that we build with them—and the more likely we are to make the discoveries that lead to better clinical outcomes.

The more we can understand the patient perception of the quality of care delivered, the better we can drive outcomes that impact results.

The Survey Questions

This aspect of the HCAHPS survey asks patients about their perception of nursing care during their hospital stay. Answers are given in frequency scale: *never, sometimes, usually,* or *always*. The percent of patients who respond *always* is publicly reported on www.hospitalcompare.hhs.gov.

1. **During this hospital stay, how often did nurses treat you with courtesy and respect?**

2. **During this hospital stay, how often did nurses listen carefully to you?**

3. **During this hospital stay, how often did nurses explain things in a way you could understand?**

In the chapters that follow, we will share the two to three specific tactics for each question that positively impact the likelihood that patients will answer *always* to all three questions in the Nursing Communication composite.

This is not a laundry list of all possible tactics. Rather, it conveys a few carefully targeted specific actions you can take to immediately impact patient perception of how well your nurses communicate.

CHAPTER THREE:

COURTESY AND RESPECT (A GOAL FOR NURSES AND *ALL* STAFF MEMBERS)

THE HCAHPS QUESTION: During this hospital stay, how often did nurses treat you with courtesy and respect?

...AND THE TACTICS THAT MAKE "ALWAYS" RESPONSES MORE LIKELY

This question really addresses how successful we are at treating patients and their family members as individuals. It requires us to move from providing "task-oriented" care to holding memorable conversations and creating meaningful personal connections. In other words, we must take the time to find out what is important to a particular patient and fully partner with her and her family in the care we provide.

While this question specifically singles out nurses, everyone in the organization owns the results. Remember, patients frequently consider any staff member who is not a physician a nurse.

Based on research from our national learning lab, Studer Group has identified two tactics that, when applied and customized appropriately, will have the most impact on improving staff members' ability to show courtesy and respect to patients. They're described below:

Tactic 1: Nurse Leader Rounding on Patients

This tactic allows nurse leaders to regularly connect with patients to reinforce care, verify nursing behaviors, and recognize staff members. It is one of the most important actions you can implement to improve patient perception of courtesy and respect and of nurse communication as a whole.

While we know there is no silver bullet, organizations have documented that when this tactic is implemented, it has been shown to increase patient perception of nurse communication quickly and profoundly. We know that when patients' perception of their care is higher, they feel a sense of partnership with nurses and other staff members and are more likely to be compliant with care.

Figure 3.1

Conversation Flow:
Nurse Leader Rounding on Patients

Rounding on Patients	Greeting/Introduction
	Manage Up Staff
	Question Regarding Team Focus
	Ask About Outstanding Staff
	Thank You
	"I Have Time" Closing Question

Four Goals for Leader Rounds on Patients

1. Manage the Patient's Expectations

"Good morning, I am Faye Sullivan, manager on this unit. I stopped by to visit you. Is this a good time? I want to check in and make sure that you are receiving very good care. That is my expectation for all of our patients." Goal: Establish empathic, compassionate rapport.

2. Service Recovery

"How well are we doing in providing care?"

3. Harvest Recognition/Manage Up

"I see XXX is your (nurse, nursing assistant, or physician)." (Manage up this professional.) "Is there anyone who stands out as having provided very good care?" If the patient says everyone has been great, then ask, "Can you give me an example of how we have provided you very good care?"

4. Manage Staff Performance
Observe for/question patient about:
Quality of care: Is the patient clean, comfortably positioned, pain free? Is staff rounding hourly? Does patient know plan of care for day? Does patient know staff members' names, etc.?
Other shifts: Ask about nights, weekends, etc.
Safe environment: Make sure side rails are up,

floor is clear, arm band is in use, IV tubing and labeled meds are left at bedside, and whiteboards are complete. Also make sure Hourly Rounding^SM logs are complete and staff and MD hand washing is observed by patient.

Daily Public Recognition

"Karen, I've rounded on three of your patients today. All three know your name and their plan of care for the day. Every room is safe and clean, and whiteboards are filled out. **THANK YOU** for making it happen!"

Here are some tips to help you implement nurse leader rounding—and to emphasize courtesy and respect:

Before You Round...

- **Communicate the impact of leader rounding with staff members. (Share the *why*.)** If information about this tactic is not explained to staff in advance, they may think that the leader is checking up on them. Once they understand the impact—that their patients feel better and they may even get some recognition—they're far more likely to fully engage in the process. Promise you will follow up post-rounding for reward and recognition and closing of any performance gaps.

- **Round on staff before you round on patients.** Ask staff for any insight and information you should know prior to visiting the patient. This helps you, the leader, be better prepared and demonstrates teamwork. It also reduces the patient's anxiety and increases his confidence that his nurses and the nurse leader are on the same page regarding his care.

As You Round...

- **Let the patient know why you are there.** The patient can feel caught in the middle if he doesn't know why the nurse leader is visiting.
  - "Hi, I'm Michelle. I am the nursing director on this unit. My job is to make sure that we take excellent care of you."

  This will calm the patient and let him know nothing bad has happened.

- **Show courtesy and respect by asking questions.** Ask the patient questions that confirm partnership in his care.
  - "How are we doing keeping you informed about what is going on?" "How are we doing at managing your pain?" "What did the nurses discuss when they were together at shift change?"

- **Manage the patient's expectations.**
  - "Good morning. I'm Faye, a manager on the unit. I like to visit with each of our patients on this unit for about five minutes daily. Is this a good time? I want to check in and make sure we are keeping you updated. How are we doing at communicating with you regularly? We should be checking in hourly; is this happening?"

- **Make the questions actionable.** Asking open-ended questions like, "How has the care been?" can reduce efficiency. As a rule of thumb, a question that is asked generically will often get a generic answer like "fine." But if a question is asked specifically, the patient will often provide specific feedback that is then actionable. Design questions to gain specific valuable information, such as, "Do you know your plan of care for the day?"

- **Manage up the nurse.** Let the patient and the patient's family know about the providers caring for him.
  - "I see Mary is your nurse. She has been with us for 10 years and is often mentioned as a favorite by her patients."

  This will let the patient know he is in good hands.

- **Harvest recognition.** Ask the patient if there is anyone you should recognize who has provided extra-special care. Ask for specific examples. After leaving the patient's room, take a moment to publicly recognize any staff member he mentioned. This will make that staff member feel great and also let others know the behaviors you are looking for. Pay particular attention to comments that reflect a culture of courtesy and respect.

- **Say thank you and ask the "I have time" closing question.** Thanking the patient for his time goes a long way toward helping him feel respected. Don't forget to say, "Is there anything I can do for you? I have time." If you don't assure the patient that you have time, he may assume you're too busy (but he'll still hit the call light later).

After You Round...

- **Recognize the staff.** Publicly recognize staff members who have done a good job.
    - "Ashley, I've rounded on four of your patients today. All of them stated that you have been visiting them every hour and taking the time to make sure they are fully informed. We are focusing on improving the patients' perception of our communication, and you have set an excellent example. Thank you."

- **Coach for improvement.** From time to time, patients will share negative feedback. Your response should be twofold: 1) address the issue in an appropriate manner, and 2) follow up with the patient to let him know you dealt with it and to ensure that the problem isn't continuing. Perform any service recovery as appropriate.

- **Realize leader rounding is all about consistency. Make it a part of your daily routine.** Rounding is extremely impactful, but it must be done consistently. Use a rounding log and build times into your schedule to round.

Tactic 2: Focus on Acknowledging the Patient and Introducing Care Providers (the "A" & "I" of AIDET℠)

When patients enter the hospital, they are generally anxious and scared. Sometimes they're in pain. About half of them came from the ED and didn't even expect to be in the hospital. They have no control over where they stay, what they wear, and who is caring for them.

As a care provider, you can take specific steps to help patients become more engaged in their own care. At the same time, you can build positive relationships and reduce patient anxiety.

You make an impression on the patient starting the minute you walk into the room. Remember, she is scared, doesn't know you, and is anxious to find out what you're going to do. The first two letters in the communication framework of AIDET—which stand for Acknowledge and Introduce—help you alleviate these problems.

It's proven that focusing on just the acknowledgment of the patient (and her family) and the introduction of each care provider can greatly impact her perception that she's being treated with courtesy and respect.

To improve your results in this area, train everyone who interacts with the patient to acknowledge the patient each and every time they enter the room. They should address the patient by name, and if family or visitors are in the room, greet them as well.

A few tips:

- **Knock—and wait for permission—before entering the patient's room.** This is a way to demonstrate respect just as you'd knock before entering a person's home or bedroom. Do the same for opening a curtain or approaching the bed. Ask the patient if now is a good time.

- **Acknowledge everyone in the room.** Upon entering the patient's room, perform a quick scan of visitors and family. Remember to include the family as you speak to the patient. Depending on the patient's condition, the family may be your best source of information.

- **Assure privacy.** You can quickly learn a visitor's relationship to the patient by saying, "Mrs. Lyons, I need to speak with you about your care. Is now a good time, or shall I come back when we have a bit more privacy?" Or, "Visitors are important, but I need to work with Mrs. Lyons. Would you like me to show you where you can wait? It should take us about 30 minutes." Typically the patient will state the relationship and whether it is okay to include the family member or visitor in discussions or allow them to stay in the room.

- **Make the patient priority one.** In healthcare, we are used to multi-tasking; however, doing so can make the patient feel she is *not* being treated courteously. When you first enter a room, engage fully in the conversation with the patient and family prior to completing any tasks at hand. Making eye contact, facing the patient, and carefully listening for this first part of the encounter will make a huge impact. If possible, sit down at the bedside. Sitting down can double the patient's perception of the time you spend with her.

- **Ask, "What name would you like us to call you?"** If the patient is newly admitted, take the time to ask how she would like to be addressed. This is the first step to gaining her partnership in her care and demonstrating courtesy and respect. Use words such as:
    - "Mrs. Lyons, good morning. I understand you came in through our ER last night. Please let me know what name you would like us to call you."

  Document what the patient would like to be called on her chart and the whiteboard, so other team members can address the patient as she requested.

- **Make proper introductions.** Once the patient and family have been acknowledged, anyone and everyone who interacts with the patient should introduce themselves, manage up their expertise, and share the purpose for the visit.
  - ○ "Good afternoon, Mrs. Lyons. My name is Jack, and I'm a medical technologist. I'll be drawing your blood today. I've been a medical technologist for eight years. Is there anything you need before we get started?"

- **Bring up previous meetings.** With each additional encounter with the patient, build on the connection you've already established.
  - ○ "Good morning, Mrs. Lyons. I'm Patty. I was your nurse two days ago and get to take care of you again today. I remember it was important to you to have the chaplain visit. Were you able to meet the chaplain? Can you tell me what has happened since I last saw you?"

  This will demonstrate to the patient that you care and are not just moving through steps in a process.

- **Use non-verbal communication.** Look at the patient, position yourself beside her, talk in a caring tone, and make eye contact. Use your judgment as to whether it is appropriate to touch the patient.

- **Look for non-verbal cues.** Watch to see if the patient looks down or lowers her voice as she shares information. These may be cues that indicate she is uneasy and has more information to provide. If anything is noticed, take time to sit and explore it a bit more. Slow down and make her comfortable. As your relationship improves with the patient so will your ability to accurately gauge these non-verbal cues.

- **Consider cultural sensitivities.** Each culture has its own set of expectations regarding communication. When you are interacting with patients from cultures different from your own, try to be aware and accommodating of these variations. It may be helpful to know the demographics of your community and review the cultural needs of the different groups.

Tactic 3: Use Key Words at Key Times

What are Key Words at Key Times? Basically, they are carefully chosen words healthcare professionals use to connect the dots and help patients, families, and visitors better understand what we are doing—and most importantly, *why*.

Often we *think* we've conveyed a particular message, but in reality what we thought we were communicating may not have been heard. Key words help a patient better understand his care. They help him feel more engaged in his care processes, which in turn makes him more likely to ask questions and to comply with treatment.

Key words align the behavior of the staff to the needs of the patient. They help us build mutually beneficial relationships with our patients and allow them to feel they are being treated with courtesy and respect.

Let your team be part of the process of helping to choose three to four sets of key words to demonstrate courtesy and respect. Staff will be more likely to use these words if they are part of determining what to focus on— and if they understand the impact.

Here are a few tips and examples:

- **Seek the patient's partnership in his care.**
  Use key words to set the stage for how you will meet the patient's needs and establish his role as part of the care process. Give him power and allow him to be in charge of the care he receives.
  - "Mr. Robinson, it's important to us that you feel comfortable about the care that we provide to you today. I will ask you three questions, but I want you to know that you can interrupt me at any time if you have questions. Your questions are as important as my questions."
  - "Your doctor has established these goals for your care today...Do these make sense to you?"
  - "It's important to accomplish the following things this morning...Is now a good time to start?"

- **Share what you are doing to respect his privacy, safety, etc.** If you have curtains between beds and you close them, does the patient know you are doing this to respect his privacy? He could think you are being rude or have something to hide. Use key words to ensure patient understanding and compliance with safety and privacy measures:
  - "Out of respect for your privacy, I'm going to close the curtain."
  - "One of the side effects of the medication you are on is dizziness. For your safety, I am putting up the bedrail. Is there anything I can move closer to you, so it is within reach? Please do not try to get up without assistance. Call us and we will help."
  - "Again, for your safety I want to help you get to the bathroom. Would you like to try now?"

- **Ask permission.** Always ask the patient if now is a good time, explain what you are about to do, and seek permission to move forward. If the patient hesitates to allow you to move forward, it is typically due to a lack of understanding. Seeking permission will allow you to make sure the patient understands what you are about to do and why.

- **Avoid "scale" wording.** Do not use the scale of any patient satisfaction survey as part of key words. Instead, focus on the behavior or the actual patient care.

- ○ Wrong: "We know that keeping you and your family informed is important to you. We want to make sure we always communicate well. Please let us know if you feel we are not always keeping you and your family informed."
- ○ Right: "You've shared that keeping you and your family informed is important to you. We want to make sure we're doing that. What type of information is most important to you and your family? Please let us know if you feel we missed an opportunity to share information."

- **Demonstrate response to his need.** When something goes wrong for the patient, make an effort immediately to make it right. Always apologize first and share what the next steps are. If possible, take care of the problem from the patient's room. This shows the patient you have made his priority your priority.
    - ○ Call to engineering from patient room: "Good morning, this is Carol on 3 West. I am in Mr. Robinson's room, 319, and his TV is not working. It is my priority to get this fixed. How quickly can you send someone to look at it?"

Remember, the greatest way to demonstrate respect and courtesy is to customize patient care. Using the "A" and "I" in AIDET and key words help you build a relationship with each patient. As the relationship grows, you'll be able to continue to further individualize his care. Studies have shown the more individualized a patient's care, the better his outcomes are.

Tools & Resources

Studer Group offers a variety of tools and resources that support the tactics discussed in this chapter. To access the most up-to-date offerings, please visit www.studergroup.com/HCAHPS.

Chapter Four:

Careful Listening

THE HCAHPS QUESTION: During this hospital stay, how often did nurses listen carefully to you?

...AND THE TACTICS THAT MAKE "ALWAYS" RESPONSES MORE LIKELY

When we enter a patient's room, we almost always have a checklist in our heads of what we need to accomplish. As we move through this checklist, he or she may get the impression that we are not listening. Sometimes, despite our best intentions, the patient is right. And that's a problem—when our minds are focused on our checklists, we may miss cues that could allow us to provide better care.

It is only through *actively listening* to the patient that we can build the kind of relationship to allow us to individualize his or her care to achieve the best outcomes.

This HCAHPS question addresses just how closely we are listening to our patients. Getting an *always* response requires that we not just listen but also demonstrate that we have listened and truly heard what they said.

Below you'll see different approaches to two Studer Group® tactics that you might already be using. We'll explain how staff can adapt them to show patients they are listening carefully. We've found through research that these tactics, when customized in this way, have the most impact on improving patient perceptions regarding how well nurses are listening.

Tactic 1: Individualize Care for Each Patient

As care providers, we recognize that patient anxiety can adversely impact the healing process. Therefore, we are constantly looking for ways to improve our patients' ability to engage in their care and understand their care plan. This leads to improved quality of care and perception of care.

Individualized Patient Care, or IPC, helps us understand exactly what excellent care means to each patient. As we discussed in Chapter 1, it requires care providers to frequently check back in with patients to ensure that we truly are meeting their needs. That's the very heart and soul of careful listening!

A few tips for implementing IPC to impact the "nurses listened carefully" HCAHPS question:

- **Get to know the patient as a person.**
  Assuming that the patient approves, put individualized information on the whiteboard, such as "I love
  the Cowboys." This allows staff members to notice
  her interests and interact accordingly with her.

- **Recap patient responses and concerns.**
  One of the most effective ways of demonstrating that you are listening to the patient is to recap
  important aspects of the conversation. Setting the
  expectation that you'll recap will also force you to
  listen more intently. Sharing what you heard will let
  the patient know you were listening and also ensures
  you are all on the same page.
    - "I want to make sure that I understand
      exactly what you are telling me. To make
      sure, I'd like to recap your thoughts at the
      end of our conversation."
    - "Let me make sure I heard you correctly. You
      are concerned about the side effects of the
      new medication impacting your work once
      you are discharged. Is that correct? Let me
      write this on your chart and the notepad next
      to your bed. This will remind both of us to
      make sure we address this with your physi-
      cian."

- **Update the patient whiteboard with IPC
  information.** Use this information during nurse
  leader rounds, Bedside Shift Reports[SM], and other
  interactions. Make sure every shift reviews the list of

individualized needs written on the whiteboard with the patient and updates it as needed (for example, if the patient provides new information). Review the information at discharge to determine if the patient's expectations have been met—and hopefully exceeded.

- **Sit at the bedside whenever possible.** Research indicates that sitting down increases the patient's perception that you're listening, as well as her perception of the time you spent with her.

- **Consider cultural sensitivities.** Each culture has its own set of expectations regarding communication. When you are interacting with patients from cultures different from your own, try to be aware and accommodating of these variations. It may be helpful to know the demographics of your community and review the cultural needs of the different groups.

- **Recognize the impact of family.** Due to pain, clinical condition, or medication effects, family members often act on a patient's behalf. Remember to listen to these individuals and include them in the patient's care.

Tactic 2: Use Key Words to Demonstrate That You Are Listening Carefully

Key Words at Key Times are generally used to explain the care we are providing our patients. They are most commonly used to explain why we are doing something in a way that the patient will understand. They can also be used to demonstrate to patients that we are carefully listening to them.

Below are some tips on using key words to show you are listening:

- **Explain why you are taking notes.** Patient information often needs to be documented. However, the patient may interpret your note taking as evidence that you're not listening to him. Explain to the patient and his family why you are taking notes. Also try to glance up at them periodically.
    - "Mr. Jones, it's very important that you have a say in your care. As we talk, I will be taking notes to document the points you are making."

- **Paraphrase to ensure understanding.** This helps patients see that nurses are listening to their concerns. It can also uncover opportunities to provide better care for the patient.
    - "I heard you say you were worried about who will help you at home when you are discharged. Is that correct?"

○ "To make sure I heard you correctly, let me recap what you said."

- **Manage expectations of pain.** Pain can be part of the healing process. Key words can be used to manage expectations, so a patient understands you are listening to him even though he is still feeling pain.
  - ○ "I want to make sure we are managing your pain. On a scale of 1 to 10, with 10 being the worst pain you've ever felt, how would you rate your pain? With the procedure you had, there is some pain involved in the healing process. We'd like to get your pain to a level 3 today. Would that be manageable? We can get your pain to a 1, but it wouldn't allow you to get up and walk. It is important we get you up for your healing. Let's try to get you to a level 3 and see if that feels manageable to you. Does that sound like a good plan?"

- **Ask probing questions to show you are listening.** As the patient is speaking, ask clarifying questions to learn more about him. This will demonstrate you are listening and offers an opportunity to build a better relationship with him.
  - ○ "I've heard you say several times how nervous you are about going home. Can you help me understand what is causing you to worry?"

- **Include the family.** As you are using key words to demonstrate you are listening, remember to include the family. They may be able to clarify further or remind the patient of the conversation at a later date.
  - "Mrs. Jones, I'm so glad that you're here to listen to the medication instructions we've provided your husband. Would you mind telling me the key things you heard me say? I just want to make certain everyone understands."

- **Share the goal.** Tell each patient about the goal to provide exceptional quality care and that you need his input to do this. For instance, you can say:
  - "We will take excellent care of you on our unit; what does excellent care mean to you?"
  - "What can we do to be the BEST hospital in your eyes?"

As healthcare professionals we sometimes feel we know what's best for patients or even what's important to them. IPC can serve as a gentle reminder that patients know themselves best. This process lets you align priorities based on the patient's actual input and gain his feedback and support.

By carefully listening to our patients, we are able to build relationships with them. Acknowledging the patient and his family and introducing ourselves and our skill sets along with using key words are important tactics to show the patient we are listening. Key words ease patient and family anxiety and enable us to provide better care.

Using IPC and Key Words at Key Times also shows patients and their families that you are communicating *with* them (not *at* them) and are truly listening to them, which makes it far more likely that they'll become HCAHPS *always* responders.

Tools & Resources

Studer Group offers a variety of tools and resources that support the tactics discussed in this chapter. To access the most up-to-date offerings, please visit www.studergroup.com/HCAHPS.

CHAPTER FIVE:

UNDERSTANDABLE EXPLANATIONS

THE HCAHPS QUESTION: During this hospital stay, how often did nurses explain things in a way you could understand?

...AND THE TACTICS THAT MAKE "ALWAYS" RESPONSES MORE LIKELY

Healthcare terminology can be as confusing to patients as texting lingo is to the typical grandparent. We in the industry use a lot of large words and nicknames for large words, and you probably even have your own hospital lingo. All of this exclusionary language can leave an already anxious patient feeling very alienated.

When we take the time to explain our actions to patients and their family members in a way they understand, it relieves stress and helps them partner in their care. When patients understand the *what* and *why* behind the care they are receiving, they feel better about it. And obviously, a thorough understanding means they are more likely to comply with our directives.

The only one who can define whether she understands an explanation is the patient. We so often hear, "Well, I told her three times about that already!" from a frustrated staff member. By helping staff members empathize with the patient and her stress level, we will improve the patient's perception of our communication skills.

Below are three tactics that have had the most impact with Studer Group partners to help care providers explain care to patients in a way they understand.

Tactic 1: Hourly Rounding^{SM}

Essentially, this technique means that staff members round on patients every hour from 6 a.m. through 10 p.m. and every two hours from 10 p.m. through 6 a.m. They don't merely check in on them. Instead, they practice a series of eight specific behaviors, each aimed at creating a specific desired outcome. These eight behaviors provide a structure for explaining care to the patient and create expectations for that care.

Figure 5.1

Eight Behaviors for Hourly Rounds

Hourly Rounding Behavior	Expected Results
Use opening key words	Contributes to efficiency
Accomplish scheduled tasks	Contributes to efficiency
Address Three Ps (pain, potty, position)	Quality indicators – falls, decubitis, pain management
Address additional comfort needs	Improved patient satisfaction on pain, concern and caring
Conduct environmental assessment	Contributes to efficiency, teamwork
Ask, "Is there anything else I can do for you before I go? I have time."	Contributes to efficiency; Improves patient satisfaction on teamwork and communication
Tell each patient when you will be back	Contributes to efficiency
Document the round	Quality and accountability

Consider the following to highlight the explanation of care during Hourly Rounding:

- **Verbalize your value and narrate your care.**
  As you move through the eight behaviors of Hourly
  Rounding, explain what you are doing to the patient.
  This will aid in her understanding and ease her anxiety. Let her know why the alarm went off, why you
  are checking her IV bag, why you are checking her
  blood pressure. You will put the patient at ease, build
  trust and credibility, and improve your relationship
  at the same time.

- **Make sure nursing staff understands the**
  why. Explain the entire rounding process to the

nursing staff and explain why you're doing it and why it matters. Share with them the data on how it improves various aspects of patient care—particularly those HCAHPS-specific questions and composites. As a reminder, be careful to communicate that rounding is not about achieving good HCAHPS results but *always* about improving the patient's clinical outcomes and perception of care. Done right, Hourly Rounding will also save staff time by allowing them to provide better care to patients. This is what matters to nurses!

- **Connect Hourly Rounding to appropriate core measures.** Hourly Rounding is a good opportunity to help hardwire the communication and action regarding core measure medication time requirements. For example:
  - "Ms. Garrido, your surgery is scheduled for 10 a.m. this morning. It is now 8 a.m. As you know, I check on you every hour. I'll be back again about 9 a.m., and at that time I'll give you an antibiotic to prevent infection post-surgery. I'll also spend time explaining the surgery and duration as well as answering any of your questions. Is there anything I can do for you now?"

    OR
  - "Mrs. Chan, we want to make sure that your blood sugar is managed. Every hour I will be checking your blood glucose level to ensure it

is at an appropriate level to allow you the best opportunity for healing."

- **Train ancillary and support staff on Hourly Rounding.** This is especially true in regard to the environmental assessment. For example, the lab staff will want to make sure the bedside table is within the patient's reach prior to leaving the room. When patients hear from all our staff that we are concerned about their safety, they understand they are in a safe place.

- **Reassess the "Three Ps" or "prompting" step.** If staff members are rounding, but you are not seeing positive results, the problem may be that they are not prompting with the "Three Ps." Reassess to ensure that all staff, all the time, are asking questions around pain, potty, and position: "Tell me about your pain. Are you comfortable?" It is this "prompting" that causes the decrease in the call lights and the improvement in patient perception of care. And remember to close with, "Someone will be back in an hour."

- **Call Hourly Rounding what it is.** Specifically state that you are "rounding," not just checking in. Patients often don't equate the two.

Tactic 2: Focus on the "E" in AIDET^{SM}

When used properly, AIDET is a valuable tool for helping nurses meet the criteria required for positive responses to all three HCAHPS questions in this composite. A focus on the "E" will yield significant impact on the "understandable explanations" question.

Remember, you always want patients to partner in their care. When you're explaining care to patients, that's your real goal. Therefore, think of this as a conversation with the patient and not simply a report. You want to engage him in the conversation by asking questions to make sure he understands and is working with you.

In general, explain the tests and the pain involved (be very honest), and let him know what happens next. Pause often and seek his clarification.

Here are some tips as you focus on the "E":

- **Be aware that AIDET is scalable.** AIDET doesn't need to be implemented all at once. Focus on one letter at a time. To improve patient response to this particular HCAHPS question, focus just on the "E." If you are already using AIDET, you may want to pay particularly close attention to how you are explaining the care.
  - "Good morning, Mr. Perdue. This is Nurse Patty again. You are going to go down to the Radiology Department. The transporter is going to take you down on a gurney. Okay? They will take you to the CT Department.

They'll put you on a table, and you'll move through that big machine. It looks like a tunnel. (pause) It is like taking pictures. You'll probably be gone from your room for about an hour to an hour and a half. Okay? Now when you come back to the room, you'll be able to have lunch. We'll get that ordered. Do you have any questions?"

- **Narrate the care you are providing.** As you are caring for the patient, explain what you are doing. You are already mentally noting these items. Simply saying them out loud will greatly ease your patient's worry and increase his understanding of the care you provide.
  - Wrong: As you walk into the patient room, the IV alarm is going off. You walk over to check the monitor. Shut it off. You check the bag and see it is full. Then you say, "All right, I'll check back in a little bit."
  - Right: "Hi, Mr. Rodriguez. I know this alarm can be annoying, but it is doing its job. Let me check a couple of things quickly for you. The bag looks full and your surgical site looks good. Sometimes when you bend your arm like that, the flow gets disrupted and the alarm goes off like it's supposed to. Everything looks okay, so let's just reset this alarm. Do you have any questions for me before I leave? Great. I'll check back in an hour to see

how you are doing. Is there anything I can do for you now? Thank you."

- **Agree on the patient care plan.** To help patients heal, we sometimes have to get them to do things they don't want to do, or we have to give them an extra push. Explain your actions in a way that creates a partnership. Communicate the care plan and expectations to ensure the patient understands completely his role in the contract. Show a high level of collaboration and commitment.
  - "It's important for you to walk today. I would like for you to walk to the end of the hallway. Is this something we can agree on?"
  - "Can we agree today that even though you are still uncomfortable, you will get up 'X' times?"
  - "What is your goal today?"

- **Communicate and reinforce core measures.** For example, as needed medications are given, focus on the explanation. This will reinforce the behavior for the nurse and ease the anxiety of the patient.
  - "Mr. Kennedy, I am prescribing a beta-blocker for you to take. Beta-blockers act to help slow your pulse rate and lower your blood pressure. It will help us control your symptoms and has been proven to greatly reduce the chance of having another heart attack. This medication is very important. Is

there anything that would prevent you from getting this prescription filled?"

- **Overcome staff reluctance by focusing on the *why*.** Yes, some employees will resist using AIDET and other key words. It's important to remind staff that patients really do want to know exactly what's going on and that AIDET is a platform for communicating in ways patients can understand. It reassures patients that the best possible care is being delivered. Remind them that when AIDET is used it has been shown to dramatically reduce patient anxiety and increase compliance.

Tactic 3: Bedside Shift Report^{SM}

Safe handoffs are the responsibility of every nurse. And the good news is that there is a well-defined, proven practice that enables nurses to accomplish them: the Bedside Shift Report.

Bedside Shift Report conversations help organizations avoid dropping the baton during one of the most critical patient care intervals and provide a standardized change-of-shift procedure for staff to embrace. They involve off-going nurses, oncoming nurses, and patients.

Although details vary from facility to facility, successful implementation provides a real-time exchange of information that increases patient safety (including fewer medication errors), improves quality of care, increases accountability, and strengthens teamwork. It also reaffirms what is important to the patient at every shift change.

The Bedside Shift Report improves the patient's perception of care. By being involved in this conversation, the patient not only feels more informed, he hears that he is being listened to and feels that he is a part of his care. The patient also gains confidence in his care providers by hearing them discuss his care.

A few guidelines for implementing Bedside Shift Reports into your daily routine:

- **Have nurses conduct shift reports at the patient bedside.** During Bedside Reports, the nurse reports patient information to the nurse who will assume the patient's care. (As the name suggests, this takes place in the patient's presence.) It is an effective way to transfer care, introduce the oncoming team member, and manage up his or her skills.
    - ○ "Michael has been a nurse on our unit for five years and will take great care of you when I leave."

    Don't forget to include the patient in the report. Whiteboards should be updated at this time to reflect the new caregiver names.

- **Communicate core measure information via the Bedside Shift Report.** Use the Bedside Shift Report as an opportunity to share with the patient and the oncoming nurse any necessary core measure items, such as an assessment that needs to be completed or a medication that needs to be started or stopped at a certain time.

- **Ensure that rounding by managers takes place regularly.** As nurse leaders round, they can verify that Bedside Shift Reports are being done consistently and effectively. Nurse leader rounding on patients is a great tactic for validating the Bedside Shift Report. Essentially, during rounds the nurse leader asks the patient if he has participated in meetings between the off-going nurse and the oncoming one.

- **Ask how the patients like being included in this discussion.** In our experience, patients overwhelmingly appreciate being updated on their care in this way. Taking patient comments back to staff will reinforce the value of this practice change.

- **Provide feedback to the staff on the benefits of Bedside Reporting.** They include decreased potential for errors, improved teamwork between shifts, mentoring opportunities for less tenured nurses, and improving the patient perception of care as it relates to the "nursing communication" composite on HCAHPS. This can also be tied to National Patient Safety Goal 13 about encouraging the patient's active involvement in his own care as a safety strategy.

Ultimately, Bedside Reporting is quite reassuring for patients. It keeps them well-informed and allows them to participate in their care, which in turn makes them less anxious and more compliant.

And when Hourly Rounding, thorough explanations, and Bedside Shift Reports are done properly and consistently, patients understand what nurses and other care providers have to say about their care—and *always* responses become more likely. In addition, you gain loyal customers. Not only does this allegiance lead to improvements in patients' perception of care, it also leads to better clinical outcomes!

Tools & Resources

Studer Group offers a variety of tools and resources that support the tactics discussed in this chapter. To access the most up-to-date offerings, please visit www.studergroup.com/HCAHPS.

To follow is a worksheet that will help you create a plan to improve patient perception of care in the "nurse communication" arena.

It is impossible to overemphasize the clarity and thoroughness with which nurses and, indeed, all staff members communicate. These are the interactions by which many patients will judge their entire hospital stay! Please give them the attention they deserve.

Nursing Communication Planning Sheet

HCAHPS "TOP-BOX" PERCENTILES—December 2009 Public Reporting*

	Nursing Communication Composite				
Percentile among reporting hospitals	5th	25th	50th	75th	95th
Percent of *always* responses	62	70	75	79	85

* These numbers are estimates based on historic national percentiles.

Current Nursing Communication Domain Result: _____

Converted to percentile: _____

90-Day Goal: _____ Percentile: _____

Action Plan:

Doctor Communication

When we as an industry seek to help physicians become better communicators, we need to let them know why. And we need to be clear on why this issue matters *to the physicians*. (Hint: It may not be "because of HCAHPS.")

So why is this issue so important? Well, physicians who communicate more effectively with patients are sued less frequently, have better patient clinical outcomes, have better clinical compliance with treatment regimens, have fewer 30-day readmission rates, and—of course—enjoy better patient perception of care. They also improve their reputations in their communities.

Physicians will care about all of these reasons.

Most physicians think they are communicating well. In reality, though, fewer than 20 percent of them have been trained on how to communicate with patients. The HCAHPS survey provides them with a valuable opportunity to learn the patients' perception of the care they are providing. It's up to hospital leaders to help physicians understand this reality and facilitate the necessary changes.

Improving the HCAHPS "doctor communication" composite requires positive collaborative relationships between administration and physicians. These respectful, trusting relationships will lay the foundation for a physician's willingness to partner in the tactics covered in this section of *The HCAHPS Handbook*. It needs to really be a two-way street.

It may help for leaders to assure physicians that the tactics in the "doctor communication" section of this book are well-researched and proven to be effective. Studer Group® has discovered via our national learning lab that they have a significant impact on patients' perception of care.

Best of all, these tactics don't add more work to physicians' already jam-packed schedules. Instead, they help physicians improve their effectiveness and maximize the impact of work they are already doing.

Following is a story that demonstrates the importance of patient/physician communication. It shows how getting to really know a patient can greatly impact clinical outcomes.

Roger had been a patient of mine for 10 years and was in regularly for blood pressure checks. He was a very quiet man. In order to draw him out and ensure I was getting the complete picture, I would always ask if there was anything else I should know to help care for him. By asking probing questions, I was making a conscious effort to get to know him better, and I'm glad I did.

During one visit as we sat and talked, I noticed he was a bit more hesitant than usual. As it turned out, his hesitation was masking a troubling symptom. After some time, Roger felt comfortable enough to share that he was having rectal bleeding. (My gut reaction was to think: I've been his physician for 10 years. Shouldn't I be the first person he called when these symptoms started? *Of course, I immediately reminded myself that when scary symptoms appear, it's natural for people to go into avoidance mode.)*

It turned out Roger's father had experienced the same symptoms when he was about Roger's age—and his diagnosis had been terminal. Roger was certain his prognosis was the same.

Building from our earlier relationship, I was able to talk to Roger a bit more. I wanted him to know I felt empathy for the loss of his father, understood his worry, and wanted him to be completely tested as soon as possible to figure out exactly what was causing this symptom. I listened carefully. I assured him that I had time to hear and discuss all his concerns and questions.

I am happy to report that Roger is here and fine today. The bleeding was caused by polyps that were able to be surgically removed.

I am thankful I spent a bit of extra time with Roger and engaged myself completely in the conversation. It could have been different, and Roger could have walked out anxious and thinking there was no hope. Had I not been able to convince him to act quickly, the next time I saw him those polyps could have turned into the cancer Roger was so worried about.

Knowing Roger as a person made all the difference.

- Barbara Loeb, MD

Stories like these happen every day—and not just with patients who have known their doctor for years. It's very important for doctors to fully engage with their patients. Sometimes the quality of the relationship between the two comes down to the difference between life and death—and communication is its foundation.

In the following pages, you'll learn more about how to build the kind of engaged physician/patient relationships that lead to outcomes like Roger's.

The Survey Questions

This aspect of the HCAHPS survey asks patients about care received from doctors at the hospital. Answers are given in frequency scale: *never, sometimes, usually,* or *always.* The percent of patients who responded *always* is publicly reported on this composite at www.hospitalcompare.hhs.gov.

1. **During this hospital stay, how often did doctors treat you with courtesy and respect?**

2. **During this hospital stay, how often did doctors listen carefully to you?**

3. During this hospital stay, how often did doctors explain things in a way you could understand?

This section is divided into three chapters, each based on one of the questions in the HCAHPS "doctor communication" domain. Each chapter shares two to three specific tactics that positively impact the likelihood that patients will answer *always* to the respective question.

This is not a laundry list of all possible tactics. Rather, it conveys a few carefully targeted specific actions you can take to immediately impact patient perception of how well your doctors communicate.

CHAPTER SIX:

DOCTOR COURTESY
AND RESPECT

THE HCAHPS QUESTION: During this hospital stay, how often did doctors treat you with courtesy and respect?

...AND THE TACTICS THAT MAKE "ALWAYS" RESPONSES MORE LIKELY

Patients have come to assume quality care. In fact, it has been demonstrated that the principal predictor of patients' perception of quality has little correlation to objective clinical quality markers. Patients' rating of quality is more predicted by their rating of the quality of communication between the healthcare team and the patient. (Chang, J. T., et al. "Patients' Global Ratings of Their Health Care Are Not Associated with the Technical Quality of Their Care." *Annals of Internal Medicine* 144, no. 9 (2006): 665-72.)

In the eyes of patients, core measures may not differentiate one hospital from another. Effective communication is what separates the good from the great in today's consumer healthcare marketplace. The rising premium on delivering effective communication with patients can be demanding and sometimes frustrating for physicians. Much of that frustration comes down to the reality of compressed time and patients' expectations.

The patient-centered model—characterized by patient involvement and inclusion in clinical decisions—is how care will be delivered going forward. Indeed, HCAHPS "doctor" questions are becoming a transparent verification tool for critically important physician behaviors.

While this HCAHPS question focuses on how often the patient feels doctors have communicated well with her, it's not just a doctor issue. Nurses and other care providers also impact responses to this question. After all, they are responsible for the hour-by-hour assessment and care of the patient, and the patient may not always make a clear-cut distinction between care by doctor and care by someone else. Plus, there's plenty that nurses and other care providers can do to boost the patient's perception of the physician.

This chapter focuses on tested and proven ways to improve the nurse/physician relationship to better communicate with patients. Executed properly, they can have an enormous impact on the patient's perception of courtesy and respect.

We've found the two evidence-based tactics in this chapter have the most impact on physicians' ability to show courtesy and respect to patients.

Tactic 1: Strengthen Nurse/Physician Relationships

The way nurses and physicians interact says a lot to a patient. If a patient detects a disjointed connection between members of her care team—for instance, if a nurse says something like, "The consulting doctor didn't know you were going home today," or, "Your doctor didn't tell me that"—the patient feels anxious and stressed. On the other hand, when the chain of communication is unbroken, she feels soothed and confident. She feels that she is being well cared for by a good team.

A collaborative relationship will put patients at ease. When such a relationship is in place, patients feel the atmosphere of teamwork and respect that results. Nurses are able to better keep patients informed because the doctor has kept *them* informed. This creates a safer environment for patients as well.

Like any successful team, the two caregivers have to recognize that neither can function efficiently and effectively without the other. Nurses and physicians must work together in order to provide the best possible care to patients. It has been noted that in 63 percent of The Joint Commission sentinel event occurrences, *communication breakdown is the leading root cause.*

Here are a few proven tips on fostering good nurse/physician relationships to communicate respect:

- **Foster two-way communication.** Effective communication between caregivers can strengthen a collaborative approach to care and prevent negative patient outcomes. Two-way communication demonstrates teamwork and respect for the nursing assessment and critical thinking skills.

- **Have nurses round with the physicians.**
  Nurses can truly impact the perception of teamwork between themselves and physicians by rounding *with* physicians on their patients. A nurse can hear what the physician tells the patient and then can reinforce the communication in later patient teaching opportunities. This is one of the best strategies to ensure consistent two-way dialogue between the doctor and the nurse and between both of them and the patients.

  At a minimum, it is helpful for the nurse to share his observations and assessments in a quick huddle with the doctor prior to rounds. This ensures the physician has the latest information and demonstrates teamwork to the patient. Two-way dialogue is the best way to ensure this is a seamless transition of care.

- **Use a consistent framework for communication.** One way patients assess quality is by the effectiveness and clarity of communication between the nursing staff and physicians. In order to provide collaborative care to the patient, strategic conversations must occur. When the conversations do not convey critical components or provide information needed to make decisions, the implementation and the results may fall short.

- ○ Many hospitals have adopted the evidence-based SBAR model to communicate important messages. It is highly adaptable for all important conversations that require a decision to be made and an action to be taken. SBAR is an acronym that stands for S = Situation, B = Background, A = Assessment, and R = Recommendation. While it is only a framework, it does help communicate messages in a consistent and reliable way. Physicians will appreciate this, and patients will feel like they are cared for by a collaborative team.

- **Use Got Chart.** This is a reminder for all nurses to have the chart in hand when they are calling a physician or asking a physician to make a clinical decision. It is a method for standardizing the nurse/physician information exchange so quality, safety, and efficiency are assured. It also ensures the physician has the information she needs to make a decision over the phone or before visiting the patient. (Not only does this help provide better, quicker outcomes for the patient, it demonstrates respect for the physicians—and they will notice it!)

  Here's a quick summary of how the Got Chart works. It helps you make sure you have all the information the physician might ask about before you call. Then, when you call, it reminds you to do the following:

- ○ Have at hand: medical chart, recent assessment (all recent labs with times done), list of medications, code status, and the most recent vital signs.
- ○ Enter the complete seven-digit number when paging. Or, if leaving a digital message, use all seven digits.
- ○ Inform the unit clerk of your page to ensure efficient transfer.
- ○ Identify yourself, the unit, the patient, the room number, and the admitting diagnosis.
- ○ State the reason for your call.
- ○ Document in the medical chart: to whom you spoke, time of call, and summary of conversation.

These reminders apply to the electronic medical record as well. Even though you might not have the chart in hand, it is important to be aware of and relay all relevant information the physician needs to make decisions on the plan of care.

- **Manage up when possible.** We can show courtesy and respect to our patients by sharing positive information about their other care providers. Managing up takes very little time and is proven to reduce patient anxiety and improve perception of care.

Often, patients will share these positive comments with other staff members. For instance, a patient will say to a nurse, "Dr. Jones mentioned that he is always confident and comfortable with you as his patients' nurse." Managing up can change the environment and help create a collaborative and cooperative team that works together to take great care of patients.

Here are examples to show how each care provider can manage up the other:

Nurse manages up physician: "Ms. Kind, I see Dr. Jones will be visiting you today. He is one of the best physicians at this hospital. He has been practicing for more than 20 years and has an excellent reputation."

Physician manages up nurse: "Ms. Kind, you are fortunate to have Florence as your nurse. Her clinical judgment and assessments are a real asset to our team. I feel comfortable knowing she is caring for you."

- **Use physician notepads.** These are notepads given to patients, so they can write questions to the doctors or nurses. Patients are encouraged to use the notepads to ensure they feel informed and included in their plans of care. This is a visual representation to the patient and her family that we invite their questions and involvement in her care.

  Here's how physician notepads work: As he is reviewing the care plan for the day, the nurse asks if the patient has any questions for the doctor. He then writes the questions down on the notepad and asks the patient to add any more questions as she thinks of them. (If the patient is incapacitated, the family is encouraged to write questions.)

When the doctor rounds on the patient, she can ask, "Have you had any questions since I saw you yesterday?" They can then review the questions together. If the nurse has already answered a question, it can be crossed off but left on the notepad so the doctor can see what it was. As the nurse rounds on patients, he can use the notepads as a vehicle for managing up the physician.

- ○ "Ms. Garrido, I see that Dr. Lee was here this morning. Was she able to answer all of your questions? That's good. She does such a nice job of using these notepads to ensure you feel comfortable asking questions."

- **Share schedule information with patients.** As part of setting and clarifying expectations, share as much information as possible about the physician routines. For example:
  - ○ "Mr. Woods, Dr. Jones will be making rounds tomorrow at 6 a.m. I know this is early, but he is going to surgery and wants to make sure there is no delay in your care."
  - ○ "Dr. Jones has a wonderful physician assistant who rounds early in the morning. She will usually review all the tests and have them ready for Dr. Jones to review with you when he rounds around noon."
  - ○ "Mrs. James, I know you wanted to take a shower, but I just saw Dr. Jones, and he will

be making his rounds soon. I know you will want to talk with him about the questions you wrote down, so perhaps you can wait to take your shower until after he rounds."

Of course, we do not want to set an expectation that we cannot deliver on, so ensure you just help inform the patient and do not create an expectation.

o "I know Dr. Jones told you that you could go home first thing in the morning, but let me help you understand what that means. We have to have the results of your specific lab test back, and that is usually around 10 a.m., so why don't we plan on around 11 a.m. if all goes well."

Tactic 2: Focus on Acknowledging the Patient and Introducing Care Providers (the "A" & "I" of AIDET℠)

AIDET is an acronym that represents the framework to effectively communicate with patients. AIDET has been proven to improve the patient experience but also to impact clinical outcomes. It makes patients more likely to comply with medications and treatment regimens. It helps alleviate their anxiety and fosters better compliance with discharge instructions.

Below is an example of AIDET in the context of physicians.

A—Acknowledge: How physicians greet patients and establish a first impression.

I—Introduce: How physicians and others introduce themselves to patients, their role in the patients' care, and the experience they bring.

D—Duration: Keeping the patient informed on wait times, admission length, test turnaround times, therapeutic effect, or symptom resolution.

E—Explanation: Providing patients with information on treatment, medications, diagnosis, and therapy options.

T—Thank You: Thanking patients for trusting physicians with their care and closing the clinical encounter.

The *Archives of Internal Medicine* (Arora, Vineet, et al. "Ability of Hospitalized Patients to Identify Their In-Hospital Physicians." *Archives of Internal Medicine* 169, no. 2 (2009): 199-201.) reported that 75 percent of patients admitted to the hospital were unable to name a single doctor assigned to their care. Of the remaining 25 percent who were able to give a name, only 40 percent were correct. This is a real shame. The truth is, patients want to be treated by capable clinicians who care about them. By taking a critical moment to properly introduce

A Doctor's Perspective on Those First Few Seconds

When we introduce ourselves, sharing what our role is and what our experience is, that is an effort to reduce patient worry and anxiety. It gives patients confidence in the person responsible for their care. It lets them know they are in expert hands, that the doctor is listening, and that you are going to take great care of them. In the absence of a good introduction, the first impression of a patient is really compromised. It is difficult to recover from this kind of start.

The first seconds of an interaction with the patient and family must convey clinical confidence, approachability, understanding, compassion, and kindness from a physician who genuinely cares about patients. Getting those few seconds right is a fundamental first step in the physician/patient/family interface. Most physicians agree that properly acknowledging patients is important and can significantly impact patient perception.

- Stephen C. Beeson, MD, author of *Practicing Excellence* and *Engaging Physicians* himself and the training and expertise he brings to a case, a physician shows that he cares about the patient.

The way a physician greets the patient and introduces himself (and his specialty or role in the care) will set the stage for every encounter. Done properly, it will demonstrate courtesy and respect. This, in turn, will put the patient at ease and make him comfortable enough to partner in his care. This is especially important in the inpatient setting where a patient may meet several doctors, from hospitalists, consultants, residents, and even student doctors.

Tips to further impact the "A" and "I":

Nurses Can...

- **Reinforce physicians' "A" and "I."** Care providers can re-communicate the physician's "A" and "I" to reinforce the information. Here's an example to illustrate how it works:
  - Physician: "Mr. Werner, my name is Dr. Cooper. Your primary care physician, Dr. Roberts, and I work together often. He asked me to do an assessment of your breathing today. Let me tell you a little about myself and then about the assessment. I'll share the results with Dr. Roberts by the end of the day."
  - Nurse (visiting after Dr. Cooper's visit): "Hello again, Mr. Werner. I'm Kate, and I'm stopping back to see how you are doing. I see Dr. Cooper has come in. He is one of our

best specialists in dealing with your condition. Dr. Roberts refers to him frequently. Do you have any questions that I can answer or that you want to write down for when the doctors visit you tomorrow?"

Physicians Can...

- **Be aware of relevant clinical data and communicate it to the patient.** Patients lose trust when a physician is unfamiliar with their patient information. Physicians need to communicate an awareness of relevant clinical events, consult opinions, diagnostic test results, and their own past history with the patient.

- **Knock first and ask permission to come in.** Out of simple respect, knock on the patient's door prior to entering. Allow him a few seconds to answer and prepare for your entry. Upon entry, greet the patient by name.

- **Make eye contact.** Upon entering the room, look the patient in the eye. It is also important to establish clear contact with family members and acknowledge them as well. Other important non-verbals include leaning forward, facing the patient, and using hand expressions with palms up. Sit down if possible.

- **Address the patient by name and shake hands.** An overwhelming 91 percent of patients wanted to be addressed by name. Take the time to address the patient by first and last name. Then ask him what he'd prefer to be called. Studies have shown that 78 percent of patients wanted their physician to shake hands. (Green, Marianne, Gregory Makoul, and Amanda Zick. "An Evidence-Based Perspective on Greetings in Medical Encounters." *Annals of Internal Medicine* 167, no. 11 (2007): 1172-76.)

  This is a real opportunity for all physicians. Recent studies have shown physicians use a patient's name less than 50 percent of the time during clinical encounters. (Green, Marianne, Gregory Makoul, and Amanda Zick. "An Evidence-Based Perspective on Greetings in Medical Encounters." *Annals of Internal Medicine* 167, no. 11 (2007): 1172-76.)

- **Share your name.** Studies have shown that the patient's preferred method of introduction is first and last name. This reduces formality and makes the physician more approachable. In a recent study, 68 percent of patients could not name one of their primary doctors. (O'Leary, Kevin J., et al. "Hospitalized Patients' Understanding of Their Plan of Care." *Mayo Clinic Proceedings* 85, no. 1 (2010): 47-52.)

- **Describe your exact role in the care of the patient.** The average patient can encounter nearly 30 care providers following surgical admission and 20 providers in a medical case. The absence of clear introductions can instill confusion and anxiety and can diminish trust.

- **Communicate experience and expertise.** Patients want to know that a physician has experience and that they are in competent, expert hands. If a physician explains that he has been caring for patients with similar conditions for 15 years and has treated thousands of them successfully, it reassures the patient. Not only is the patient's anxiety certainly reduced, but he also feels respected because the physician took the time to share this information with him.

- **Ask permission to begin an exam or assessment.** In any other setting it would be considered rude to invade a person's space and especially to touch him. It is a clear sign of respect to ask the patient for permission to begin the exam. Then to make the patient comfortable, narrate the exam. Let the patient know the *what* and *why* behind the exam. And, tell him the results of the physical exam when possible (i.e., "This looks normal.").

- **Sit whenever possible.** Patients perceive the amount of time a physician spends with them as an indicator of respect. Research has shown that patients involved in seated interactions overestimated the time providers spent performing exams by an average of 1.3 minutes. (Goyal, D. G., et al. "To Sit or Not to Sit?" *Annals of Emergency Medicine* 51, no. 2 (2008): 188-93.)

While the patient may perceive the time spent as longer, this alone will not compensate for other communication gaps, such as interrupting and closed body language. There is also evidence that shows that some patients assess physicians as being more compassionate when they sit at the bedside, especially when sharing bad news. (Bennett, M. I., et al. "A Randomized, Controlled Trial of Physician Postures When Breaking Bad News to Cancer Patients." *Palliative Medicine* 21, no. 6 (2007): 501-5.)

- **Change of plane.** When physicians change the plane of the conversation, it can seem like a transition to a new conversation. For example, a physician may stand when he walks in and greets the patient, sit at the bedside when he is listening to the patient history, stand to assess the patient, and sit in a chair to talk about the assessment. The patient will perceive there to be four distinct parts to the exam. This may feed into the perception that physicians who sit spend more time with patients. In any event, sitting at the bedside demonstrates respect and tells the patient, "I have time for you."

How physicians communicate with patients is a critical component of care. It's very important that patients feel respected. When physicians and nurses work collaboratively to demonstrate courtesy and respect—and when physicians learn a few key words and easy-to-implement tips—everyone wins. The patient feels good about his experience, and doctors and staff are able to provide the best possible care.

Tools & Resources

Studer Group offers a variety of tools and resources that support the tactics discussed in this chapter. To access the most up-to-date offerings, please visit www.studergroup.com/HCAHPS.

CHAPTER SEVEN:

CAREFUL LISTENING
BY DOCTORS

THE HCAHPS QUESTION: During this hospital stay, how often did doctors listen carefully to you?

...AND THE TACTICS THAT MAKE "ALWAYS" RESPONSES MORE LIKELY

According to Dr. Jerome Groopman, author of *How Doctors Think*, physicians interrupt their patients within 18 seconds of the start of the conversation. Listening counts. It counts even more than having access to the latest technology and most sophisticated equipment. It is through carefully listening to what the patient is saying that we provide the best care and create a meaningful patient/physician relationship.

Studer Group examined the evidence we gathered via research in our national learning lab and identified two tactics that have the most impact on improving patients' responses to the "doctors listen carefully" HCAHPS question. They are as follows:

Tactic 1: Reflective Listening (Paraphrasing)

Reflective listening, also known as parallel talk and paraphrasing, is a critical physician skill. It involves paying close attention to what you are hearing, so you can repeat it back to the speaker. When you practice this skill, you convey to the patient that you are listening and that you care about getting the story right.

Reflective listening can accomplish all of the top six attributes patients want in physicians (Harris Poll. 2004.). These attributes are listed in order below. *I want my physician to:*

1. Treat me with dignity and respect
2. Listen carefully to my health concerns
3. Be easy to talk to
4. Take my concerns seriously
5. Be willing to spend enough time with me
6. Truly care about me and my health

Tips for using reflective listening:

- **Pay attention to your tone of voice.** Take a few deep breaths to calm your pace prior to talking with patients. Slow down and use a calm, even tone. You'll come across as unrushed and interested. One study found voice tone alone could differentiate nomalpractice claim surgeons from high-claim ones.

High-claim surgeons were judged to be dominant, fast-paced, and less concerned for patients compared to no-claim surgeons. (Ambady, Nalini, et al. "Surgeons' Tone of Voice: A Clue to Malpractice History." *Surgery* 132, no. 1 (2002): 5-9.)

- **Use open-ended questions.** Open-ended questions are designed to encourage full, meaningful answers using the patient's own knowledge and/or feelings. They allow physicians to gather as much information as possible. For example, if a patient comes in with chest pains, the physician would say, "Tell me about your chest pain." A closed question would be, "Where exactly is your chest pain?" This pulls only limited information from the patient.

   Open-ended questions open the door and convey to the patient, "Okay, this physician is listening to me."

- **Follow the two-minute rule.** After an open-ended question is asked, allow the patient to talk for at least two minutes uninterrupted. Maintain eye contact for 80 percent of the encounter. (You'll need to practice this; it is very difficult to allow someone to talk for two minutes uninterrupted…but it is an important habit to master when you're striving to listen carefully.)

- **Paraphrase with key words.** Key words are phrased to evoke a predictable positive impression.

Here are some examples of key words to demonstrate listening.
- "I want to make sure I heard you correctly..."
- "I care about how you are doing..."
- "Let me see if I understand..."
- "Does that sound reasonable to you?"

Tactic 2: Demonstrate Empathy

Physicians certainly feel empathy for their patients. Unfortunately, many rarely demonstrate it. In fact, statistics show that, without training, less than 10 percent of empathetic opportunities are conveyed to patients. When patients believe you feel their pain, so to speak, they also believe you're hearing them. The two go hand-in-hand.

The truth is, the expression of empathy is a conscious behavior. The physician who chooses to seize an empathic opportunity can make a critical difference in a patient's perception of him. It can lead a patient to think, *Wow, this physician cared about me, listened to me, and treated me with respect!*

Let's say, for example, that a patient who had a big summer trip planned comes in with chest pain and finds herself in the ICU with an acute MI. After gathering the patient's history, the physician might just acknowledge the patient's personal situation: "I'm so sorry you are here and not enjoying that fun vacation you planned. I'm sure this must be really, really tough. We're going to do everything we can to take care of you."

Demonstrating empathy takes virtually no time, and it can make a big difference in the patient's perception of whether the physician is listening. When opportunities aren't seized, the patient thinks, *That doctor didn't care about me as a person. He didn't listen to a thing I said. What a jerk!*

Regardless of how a patient may interpret it, she really means there was no connectivity. When you as a physician can build that connectivity—that trust—then you have the ability to influence and impact patient decisions and compliance, driving positive clinical outcomes. If the patient does not trust you, then your ability to guide her and her family to do the right thing in terms of her medical care is compromised.

Empathy diffuses tension and fear. It says, *I understand. I care.* Empathy creates the space for the comfort in asking questions. Questions promote dialogue. And dialogue promotes a better understanding of the patient's real concerns and expectations and leads to increased compliance with physician orders.

While empathy may sound like a soft science, it isn't. It's about building the ability to have influence over what patients do clinically. It's about earning trust—which is the ultimate commodity in a physician/patient relationship.

A few tips for showing empathy:

- **Imagine yourself in the patient's shoes.** As you listen place yourself in that situation. You are now in a strange place, surrounded by people you don't know, possibly undressed, and likely scared and in pain. It is one of the most vulnerable situations you can ever be in. Picture this happening with you and your family. How would you be feeling?

- **Say, "I'm sorry."** You can't always understand exactly what a patient is experiencing, but you can always tell her you are sorry she is in that situation, feeling this pain, or experiencing such loss.

- **Actively listen.** Completely engage yourself in listening. Practice the 60/40 rule: listen 60 percent of the time and talk 40 percent. Hear the words but also try to feel the emotion the patient is showing. Be aware of the non-verbal signs she is showing.

- **Offer help or a suggestion.** Put the patient at ease with key words that offer a solution or at least move her toward a solution. "I am so sorry you are spending your birthday in pain in the hospital. Let me start by helping to reduce the pain you are feeling."

- **Recognize the impact of family.** Due to pain and medication effects, family members often act on a patient's behalf. Remember to listen to them and include them in the patient's care.

Sometimes it feels like listening—*really* listening—is a lost art. The same is true of showing empathy. The good news is that the two can go hand-in-hand—and doctors are in the perfect position to practice both. When we listen and show empathy, we not only build stronger relationships with our patients, we gain clues that help us provide proper diagnoses and better care.

Tools & Resources

Studer Group offers a variety of tools and resources that support the tactics discussed in this chapter. To access the most up-to-date offerings, please visit www.studergroup.com/HCAHPS.

CHAPTER EIGHT:

DOCTOR EXPLANATION OF CARE

THE HCAHPS QUESTION: During this hospital stay, how often did doctors explain things in a way you could understand?

...AND THE TACTICS THAT MAKE "ALWAYS" RESPONSES MORE LIKELY

How well do doctors explain critical issues to their patients? Studies suggest the answer is often *not very*.

One Mayo Clinic study suggests that 58 percent of patients discharged from the hospital don't know their own diagnosis. Another study states "a substantial number of hospitalized patients do not understand their care plan. Patients' limited understanding of their plan of care may adversely affect their ability to provide informed consent for hospital treatments and to assume their care after discharge." (O'Leary, Kevin J., et al. "Hospitalized Patients' Understanding of Their Plan of Care." *Mayo Clinic Proceedings* 85, no. 1 (2010): 47-52.)

These findings certainly provide a strong call to action to do better in educating patients and giving them information regarding their own conditions.

To achieve this goal, physicians need to do three things:

1. Explain the patient's diagnosis in really clear simplistic terms.

2. Explain medications to the patient in a way that shares the name of the medication, the purpose of the medication, how long he is going to be taking the medication, and what the potential side effects are.

3. Confirm that the information the patient is provided is helpful and that he understands it. Ask, "Is there any more information you need?"

This HCAHPS question gives physicians an opportunity to see how well we are explaining our care to patients in a way they understand. It is a frequency question that reflects how often doctors explained things in ways patients could understand.

Below is one tactic that will help improve outcomes in this area:

Tactic 1: Focus on the "E" in AIDET℠

As we've already discussed, AIDET is an acronym that represents the framework for effective communication with patients. It has been proven to not only improve the patient experience but also impact more clinical outcomes. Patients are more likely to comply with medications and treatment regimens and follow the recommendations of their care providers. They have less anxiety and better comply with the care plans as outlined in their discharge instructions.

And (as we've also mentioned previously) AIDET is the foundation for meaningful dialogue and should not be thought of as an initiative that should be implemented all at once. Key elements can be focused on to drive outcomes in the area needed. If data analysis indicates the question with the most opportunity for improvement is the explanation of care, the obvious choice would be to zero-in on the "E."

Explanation involves providing the patients with information on treatment, medications, diagnosis, and therapy options in ways they can understand. Explaining clinical information to patients is at the core of quality and safety. In the following pages, we'll specifically provide tips on *diagnosis* and *medications* as these are key areas in patients' perceptions of understandable explanations.

Area 1. Diagnosis

The quality of information patients receive and the level of understanding they have regarding their diagnosis and treatment plan can improve adherence to treatment regimens. Yet, a study by JAMA (Braddock, Clarence H. III, et al. "Informed Decision Making in Outpatient Practice: Time to Get Back to Basics." *JAMA* 282, no. 24

(1999): 2313-20.) reported that 91 percent of patients did not participate in decisions regarding treatment plans. A clear *explanation* of the diagnosis will help patients partner in their care and improve their perception that their physicians explained things in a way they understood. It will also help maximize patient compliance and create more positive outcomes.

Here are some tips physicians can use to better explain diagnoses and gain patient partnership in their care plans:

- **Provide diagnosis in a clear order.** It is important not to jump around when doing this. Provide the information in the following order with clear transitions:
    1. Share the diagnosis OR what you are attempting to clarify or rule out.
    2. Share the recommendations for treatment.
    3. Share the expected clinical course of the condition.
    4. Explain what the patient needs to do.
    5. Address symptom management.

- **Share the name of the diagnosis.** Patients want to know what they have. Let them know the name and write it out for them. If you are not certain, then provide a list of possibilities based on presenting symptoms and exam findings. Equally important is talking about the serious diseases they *don't* have. In other words, reassure patients that they are not dying. Many people tend to anticipate the worst-case scenario. If you can alleviate that fear, it's best to do so.

- **Use language the patient understands.** Medical terminology is acceptable but must also be followed by a clear explanation of what the terms mean. Use appropriate terms. If you are talking about side effects, say side effects. (Too often, physicians just say, "Look for this," or, "Call me if this happens," rather than actually calling the symptoms side effects.)

- **Let him know about diagnostic testing.** If there is a list of diagnostic possibilities and further information is needed to clarify the diagnosis, physicians should explain this to patients. Explain the nature of the test, what will be done, what specifically is being looked for. Let the patient know how long the test will take, if it will be noisy, if there will be pain, or if it may be uncomfortable. Give him as much information as possible to prepare him. Don't forget to share how long it will take for the results to come back.

- **Share the recommendations for treatment.** Provide a clear summary of the treatment plan. Let the patient know what will happen next. What tests are needed? What are you looking for or ruling out? Are there any appointments or other physician consults? Be clear and thorough.

- **Share the clinical course of the diagnosis.**
  Patients want to know what they should expect.
  They will need to know the timing of a therapeutic
  improvement and if and when things will get better.
  Patients value this information, even if it isn't what
  they want to hear.

- **Share the information several times.** We
  often need to hear information several times to gain
  a complete understanding and retention. Share
  information *multiple times* and *in multiple ways*. It may
  trigger a new question from the patient that will help
  gain his compliance in his care.

- **Provide written information on the
  diagnosis.** This should include a simple explanation of the condition, self-treatment responsibilities,
  and side effects or symptoms to look out for. The
  earlier in the hospital stay you give this information
  to the patient, the better. Encourage the patient to
  read and highlight information he doesn't understand (or may need to reference later) so it can be
  discussed and clarified.

- **Ask the patient if he understands.** Patients
  are not likely to ask questions unless given an opportunity to do so. Use key words such as, "We want to
  make sure that you really understand your diagnosis
  and your medications. Is there any more information
  we can provide to you?" Allow the patient the opportunity to say, "I don't really understand what that

red pill is again. What is that for?" and give him the opportunity to say, "I've got it and I understand." If you're not certain the patient understands, ask probing questions until you can see that he does.

- **Ask for the patient's partnership.** A patient will have better outcomes if he is an active participant in his care. Gain his input. Ask, "Are you comfortable with this treatment plan? Is this something you are okay with? I want to make sure that you're okay with these recommendations."

- **Show empathy.** Place yourself in the patient's shoes. If it's appropriate, let him know you are sorry about what he's going through.

Area 2. Medications

How and what a physician says to a patient about a medication can heavily impact the probability that he will take the medication properly and completely. Studies have shown that physicians do not consistently provide the most basic medication information to patients. One study reported that 26 percent of physicians failed to mention the name of the new medication. The same study also reported that 66 percent of physicians failed to tell the patient how long to take the medication. (Hays, Ron D., et al. "Physician Communication When Prescribing New Medications." *Archives of Internal Medicine* 166, no. 17 (2006): 1855-62.)

A clear *explanation* of the medication will help patients partner in their care and improve their perception that their physician explained things in an understandable way. Not surprisingly, doing this well will also impact the HCAHPS Communication of Medications composite.

Here are some tips to explain medications and gain patient compliance:

- **Share the name of the medication.** Tell the patient the name and write it out for him. If there is another common term or abbreviation for the medication, share that with him also.

- **Share the purpose of the medication.** When the patient is aware of the intent of the medication, it improves long-term compliance. Let's say you're prescribing an antibiotic and it should be taken for seven days. Explain to the patient: "You may feel better by day four. However, in order to get rid of the infection completely, you must take the medication for seven days. So, don't stop early. Take it all."

- **Let him know the duration of treatment.** Failure to communicate the length of time a patient is to be on a medication may cause him to stop taking it when the first prescription runs out. This is especially problematic if it is meant to be a long-term medication. Communicate what to do if he misses a dose or if he is delayed in taking a dose.

- **Explain why.** Let the patient know why you selected this particular medication.

- **If possible let the patient choose.** Go through the choices and ask for patient input. For instance, ask, "Would you rather have a pain pill or shot?"

- **Call potential side effects what they are.** Share potential side effects with the patient. He should be told what side effects to look for and given instructions on what to do if he experiences any, including stopping the medication. This will help decrease patient-initiated discontinuation rates. Again, use the term "side effects." If you just say, "Watch out for..." or, "Make sure to call us if you see this..." the patient may not understand the importance or know what to expect.

  It is important to let the patient know that in the event of side effects that there are other treatments he can use to get well. A patient may tolerate a very painful side effect because he thinks the alternative is much worse. Let him know there are options if this medication is not tolerated.

- **Ask the patient if he understands.** Ask, "Is there any more information you need on this medication?" Give him the opportunity to answer. Respond to his questions until he is able to state that he understands.

- **Create a collaborative environment.** Make sure you ask, "Are you comfortable with this treatment plan? I want to make sure that you're okay with these medications." Sometimes patients will have an unspoken fear/reservation/uncertainty about a recommendation. If this is unresolved, they leave the hospital and just don't get the medication filled or comply with treatment.

- **Give patients a central location for important information.** Some of Studer Group's highest achievers keep a folder at the patient bedside. On the front of this folder is a spot to write down new medications along with side effects to look for. Giving patients a simple tool like this will go a long way toward helping them keep track of their medications and all the information associated with them.

When a doctor focuses on providing a thorough explanation of diagnoses and medications, his or her patients are more likely to understand their conditions and their own roles in treating them. This will lead to better compliance and better clinical outcomes. Plus, it will give patients a more favorable impression of the physician—and most likely, by extension, your hospital.

Tools & Resources

Studer Group offers a variety of tools and resources that support the tactics discussed in this chapter. To access the most up-to-date offerings, please visit www.studergroup.com/HCAHPS.

Following is a worksheet that will help you create a plan to improve patient perception of care in the "doctor communication" arena.

Once you put the tactics you've learned in this section into place, not only may your HCAHPS results improve right along with patient care, your entire staff is likely to enjoy stronger, more rewarding relationships with your physician partners. And that will benefit your organization in immeasurable ways.

Doctor Communication Planning Sheet

HCAHPS "TOP-BOX" PERCENTILES—December 2009 Public Reporting*

			Doctor Communication Composite		
Percentile among reporting hospitals	5th	25th	50th	75th	95th
Percent of *always* responses	70	76	80	83	89

* These numbers are estimates based on historic national percentiles.

Current Doctor Communication Domain Result: _____

Converted to percentile: _____

90-Day Goal: _____ Percentile: _____

Action Plan:

Section Three:

Responsiveness of Staff

P atients come to the hospital expecting good clinical care. They don't come to the hospital expecting to get sicker or to become the victims of a medical error (even though they've probably read about both kinds of occurrences in the paper). Simply providing great clinical care is not going to win you accolades in the eyes of patients because they expect it, and it does not create a memorable experience.

In part, patients equate quality care with responsiveness and courtesy. How you treat them is inextricably connected to how they perceive the care you provide.

Let's place ourselves in the patient's shoes. He is talking with a family member when his alarm goes off. The patient and his family member both quickly look to the alarm thinking, *oh no!* They hit the call button and wait and wait. In fact, they wait for four minutes. Then the nurse comes in and shuts the alarm off saying, "It was nothing." But from the patient's perspective, was it *really* nothing?

When we work in healthcare, we become accustomed to the noise of alarms and call lights. They blend in with the everyday noises of the hospital. But, just try hopping into a patient bed and listen to the alarm. See how long it takes for you to feel anxious and to want it shut off. It's a safe bet that it will take under four minutes, probably even under one minute. Now couple the jarring noise with the feeling the alarm means something (and we know it can), and you can imagine how it feels to be the patient, waiting and worried.

In this case, being responsive might mean a) getting to the patient's room much faster and b) reassuring him with a few key words that let him know what happened and that show empathy for any anxiety the alarm might have caused.

To be truly responsive to patients, it's important to demonstrate that you're making their care a priority. Individualized Patient Care, which unfolds through tactics like Hourly Rounding^{SM}, allows you to understand what "responsiveness" means to each patient and his family.

It's important to note that patient needs don't always happen when they are in their beds in their hospital rooms. Responsiveness isn't limited to nurses. If a patient has to wait two hours for her scheduled surgery or she has to wait 45 minutes for a transporter to return her from radiology after her test, this will impact this composite. This means ancillary and support service departments can have a tremendous impact on this composite.

It's important to make sure *all* patient caregivers realize that they have a responsibility to be sensitive to and respond to these needs.

When the nursing staff and ancillary departments work together, it's a combination that can't be beat. And the winner is the patient.

Here is a story that illustrates the impact of responsiveness. It was shared by a nursing director as she rounded with a nurse:

We went into this young man's room. His name was Akeem and he was about 26. His nurse Candace introduced me and explained that we were rounding together.

"Tell us a little about how your day is going," said Candace.

"Well, it's been pretty good," he responded.

"Just pretty good—it's not excellent?" Candace pressed.

"Oh no, no, it's been excellent."

"Why is that?"

"I gotta tell you, I don't know what's going on in this hospital, but this is my second time here," said Akeem. "Last time I got taken care of, but it's so much different now. When I hit my call light, it's almost like they know I am going to hit it because they are in the room right away. It's like they have ESP."

(Let me jump in here and explain that Studer Group had helped the hospital implement Hourly Rounding in the interim between Akeem's first and second stays.)

"That's good. Who's been so good to you?" asked Candace.

"Josh."

"Why is that?"

"Well, because he comes in and checks on me every hour like clockwork, and he tells me what is going on. It's almost like déjà vu. Like I said, I go to hit that light and in comes Josh to check on me."

"It sounds like we have been keeping you informed and keeping right on top of things," noted Candace.

"Absolutely!" the patient beamed.

It was clear Akeem felt cared for. The key? Responsiveness. We were able to immediately let Josh know the difference he was making.

- Shawnda, Nursing Director

When we are responsive to patient needs, we are demonstrating that we understand what is important to them. We are demonstrating that we care. When we practice the tactics that show responsiveness, we can have entire hospitals full of patients as happy as the one described above.

The Survey Questions

This aspect of the HCAHPS survey asks patients about their perception of the responsiveness of staff during their hospital stay. Answers are given in the frequency scale: *never, sometimes, usually,* or *always.* The percent of patients who responded *always* is publicly reported on www.hospitalcompare.hhs.gov.

Screening Question: During this hospital stay, did you need help from nurses or other hospital staff in getting to the bathroom or in using the bedpan?

1. **How often did you get help in getting to the bathroom or in using a bedpan as soon as you wanted?**

2. **During this hospital stay, after you pressed the call button, how often did you get help as soon as you wanted it?**

In the chapters that follow, we will share how to incorporate responsiveness to bathroom needs and call lights into Individualized Patient Care and Hourly Rounding. We'll also discuss one other specific tactic that involves the entire hospital staff responding to the patient.

This is not a laundry list of all possible tactics. Rather, it conveys a few carefully targeted specific actions you can take to immediately impact patient perception of how well your hospital staff responds to their needs.

CHAPTER NINE:

BATHROOM ASSISTANCE

THE HCAHPS QUESTION: How often did you get help in getting to the bathroom or in using a bedpan as soon as you wanted?

...AND THE TACTICS THAT MAKE "ALWAYS" RESPONSES MORE LIKELY

Imagine that you are a patient lying in bed and have to use the restroom. How long will you wait, wondering when someone is going to come in and help, before you take the risk and try it on your own? Probably not long, right? Well, your patients are no different. They will eventually take risks to get to the restroom, reach the phone, or even walk out into the hallway looking for someone to get them some pain medication.

When they take these risks, serious injuries can occur—injuries that adversely impact clinical outcomes and, obviously, patient perception of care. What's more, such injuries are financially costly.

Depending on which study you're reading, the average fall can cost anywhere from just under $4,000 to $11,000. It's true that Medicare has not reimbursed hospitals for these costs for some time. But now as a result of the Patient Protection and Affordable Care Act, hospitals failing to meet certain hospital-acquired condition (HAC) performance criteria (including falls) will be subjected to a new reimbursement penalty.

The following tactics have been proven by Studer Group® partner hospitals across the country to have the greatest impact on patients' perception that they received help as soon as they wanted it.

Please note that while this question focuses specifically on bathroom assistance, the tactics below will overlap with those of the call button assistance chapter. From the patient's perspective and hopefully yours as well, it's all about responsiveness (and not necessarily the exact wording of the question).

As a reminder, while the questions specifically refer to call button and bathroom needs, the patient may not answer *always* to the question about responsiveness if other interactions are not timely. For example, if the patient has been discharged, her ride is ready, and she has to wait for written discharge instructions, she might not think the staff always responded in a timely manner.

Tactic 1: Address Bathroom Needs During Individualized Patient Care Implementation

Individualized Patient Care (IPC) actually begins at the time of the admission assessment when we ask the patient what excellent care and communication means to her. It continues on throughout the patient's stay, integrated in all interactions such as daily rounds, at shift changes, at the time of discharge, and then again during post-visit phone calls.

It's more than just understanding the patient's thoughts, however. It's about how best to communicate that you understand, how to connect with the patient, and, ultimately, how to provide the best care. It's also about frequently assessing your own progress in providing what the patient perceives to be excellent care.

Figure 9.1

How to Implement Individualized Patient Care

Action
1. Use key words.
2. Note items on the whiteboard.
3. Ask during daily rounds.
4. Ask at shift change.
5. Ask at discharge.
6. Review the survey tool.
7. Make discharge phone calls.

IPC provides an opportunity to alleviate situations that may create unnecessary anxiety and detract from the healing process. Uncertainty around whether a patient's bathroom needs are going to be met—for instance, whether she is going to get there in time—is such a situation.

When you establish a relationship of trust and comfort, you help the patient to feel at ease and dispel worries that she may be left waiting for someone to help with her needs. Here are some tips to help you implement Individualized Patient Care—and to emphasize responsiveness regarding bathroom needs:

- **Explain the risks of unassisted bathroom visits.** Let patients know that you are offering to help them with their bathroom needs because you want to keep them safe.
  - ○ **Assess the risk and inform the patient.** Her risk of falling can change throughout her stay due to a procedure or new medication. If the risk has changed, explain why it's changed and what it means for her.
  - ○ **Seek partnership.** Ask the patient to become a partner in her care by actively taking part in the fall prevention protocol. By placing her in charge of making sure she gets help to the restroom prior to being transported to a different area, you are helping her take an active role in her care.
  - ○ **Link bathroom risks to side effects.** If a medication will cause the patient to have to use the restroom frequently or has the potential to make her dizzy, proactively offer to address her restroom needs right away.
    - "I know you said you don't really have to go to the restroom, but this medication can make you feel dizzy. We don't want to bother you after the medication takes effect, so it might be safer for you to try and go now. This way you can rest comfortably and not be interrupted in an hour."

- **Use Bedside Shift Report^{SM} as a time to ask if bathroom needs are being met.** Give your report and do the handoff in the patient's presence, so she understands that you are sharing all pertinent issues regarding her care. This ensures there will be a smooth transition from one caregiver to the next. Involve the patient in the report by asking her if you covered all the important things that she wants the oncoming nurse to know.

  The handoff is an opportunity to reassess and engage the patient with regards to how the staff is responding to her bathroom needs.
  - "Tell us how we are doing in helping you to the bathroom as you need it."

  Ask engaging, open-ended questions.
  - "Is there anything else you would like Ryan to know about your care before I leave?"

- **Schedule coverage around peak times.** Identify staff to address bathroom needs, answer call lights, and respond to patients' needs during peak times, such as at shift change and at meal times. If you are going to be unavailable for longer than 15 minutes, whether it is at shift change or a need to be in an isolation room, ask a staff member to watch your rooms for call lights. It is a good practice to identify people to cross-cover responsibility and monitor rooms during busy times.

- **Keep "bathroom" items within reach.** As appropriate, ensure urinals or bedpans are within reach of all patients. Many call lights go off because a patient cannot reach a needed item. This should be part of the environmental assessment during Hourly Rounding.

- **Implement a check-before-you-go policy.** Ask nurses and staff from other departments to do a bathroom check before they take patients to another location.
  - "I'm Mike from radiology. I'm here to take you for an MRI. We are going to be gone for about two hours. Do you need to use the restroom before we go?"

  You can also ask the patient to do her own bathroom check.
  - For example, "I know you have several tests scheduled today. If someone comes by to transfer you to these, please let them know you need to use the restroom before you go."

  This way you'll have a backup system in case a staff member forgets to ask.

- **During leader rounds make sure bathroom needs are being met.** Research has proven that leader rounds are a key to verifying and validating that a behavior is being done. The leader should actively listen and ask probing questions.
  - "How well are we doing at helping you with your needs? Tell me how we are doing at

checking on you frequently to address your bathroom needs."

Tactic 2: Use Hourly Rounding to Be Responsive to Bathroom Needs

We've just discussed IPC and explained how it relates to responsiveness regarding the patient's bathroom needs. However, although we're calling IPC a tactic, it's really more of an overarching approach to patient care. Hourly Rounding is a tactic that falls under the IPC umbrella. It is during Hourly Rounding that most of the tips we covered in the IPC section above are carried out.

Hourly Rounding can have a powerful impact and can affect many components of the patient's perception of quality care. Studer Group's national call light study discovered that when participants implemented Hourly Rounding, they were able to reduce bathroom requests by 38.7 percent.

This tactic creates the expectation with the patient that someone on the caregiver team will be back to check on him every hour—and that during every visit she will ask about bathroom needs. The patient quickly comes to realize he will be asked whether he needs to use the bathroom every hour during the day. This is a critical part of the eight key behaviors that drive the most successful results from Hourly Rounding.

The result is that the patient develops a sense of trust. He knows when to expect someone to check in on him and offer bathroom assistance and is less likely to try to take care of bathroom needs on his own. He often will wait for the next Hourly Round or visit. Not only is he safer, he also perceives the staff to always be responsive.

A few tips:

- **Set the expectation with the patient.** During the admission assessment, let the patient know that one of the staff members will be checking on him hourly during the day and every two hours through the night. Use key words such as:
  - "For your safety, we do Hourly Rounds on this unit. There are several things we check on during these visits. We check your need to use the restroom and your comfort level as it relates to pain and position. We also check to make sure you have everything you need within your reach. We don't want you to have to use your call light because we check on you so frequently. If you need something in between our regular Hourly Rounds, of course we will respond to your call light in a timely manner."

- **Communicate the goal of Hourly Rounding.** Explain to patients that the goal of Hourly Rounding is to be proactive in their care and to keep them safe. The real goal is for the patient to view care as extremely responsive, perhaps even to state, "I never had to wait to go to the bathroom. I never even had to push the call light for help." It is an offensive tool (not a defensive one).

Once the implementation is hardwired, the staff will begin to see that Hourly Rounding saves time. They are not being called into patient rooms as frequently because they are addressing needs proactively.

- **Use the key words "risky behavior" with both staff and patients.** We have found that this term engages both the hospital staff and the patients. When the purpose of Hourly Rounding is explained as the best way to help a patient avoid a dangerous situation like going to the restroom on his own, staff are more likely to get on board. Using the term "risky behavior" with patients reduces the chance that they will try to go to the restroom on their own. It also explains the *why*.
  - Sample: "One side effect of the medication is dizziness. Remember, I am going to come by every hour to check and see if you need to use the restroom. While you are on this medication, going to the bathroom on your own can be risky behavior. I want to help you when you need to go, so make sure not to try to go to the bathroom on your own."

- **Combine bathroom needs with medication administration.** Some medications require large amounts of fluid or have a side effect that puts the patient in a less ambulatory state. Be aware of this and address it upfront.

- ○ "Before I give you these meds, I'd like to help you up to see if you can use the restroom. Here's why…"

Also, remember how the medications work. If you give a diuretic to a patient at 9 a.m., there is a good chance he will need to use the restroom by 9:30 a.m. Make sure and communicate this to all caregivers, so they can proactively address medication effects.

- **Be consistent and build confidence**. If you have been practicing Hourly Rounding and haven't seen your call lights fall and patient perception of care rise, look at your consistency. If Hourly Rounding is not done consistently, the patient won't trust that you'll be back when you say you will. In our national lab of partner hospitals, we have found it takes 90 percent compliance or better to have patients consistently believe we are always responsive.

  If Hourly Rounding isn't practiced consistently, the patient will lose confidence and won't trust that someone will be checking on him every hour. This leads to patients' getting up on their own and to their response on the survey that we were not always responsive.

We are able to be more responsive to patients when we truly know what is important to them. Individualized Patient Care allows us to do just that. Hourly Rounding allows us to address patients' needs proactively. This means patients aren't waiting for a long time to use the restroom or risking a fall by getting up and trying to do so on their own. By combining the two, we can help ensure that they always have as comfortable and safe of an experience as possible while they're under our care.

Tools & Resources

Studer Group offers a variety of tools and resources that support the tactics discussed in this chapter. To access the most up-to-date offerings, please visit www.studergroup.com/HCAHPS.

CHAPTER TEN

CALL BUTTON RESPONSE

THE HCAHPS QUESTION: During this hospital stay, after you pressed the call button, how often did you get help as soon as you wanted it?

...AND THE TACTICS THAT MAKE "ALWAYS" RESPONSES MORE LIKELY

Time seems to move much more slowly when you are waiting for something. Have you ever seen family members standing in the patient's doorway with worried looks on their faces? Often these families are acting as call lights. Their daughter or father or grandmother is in the room in pain or experiencing a specific need. The family is concerned and looking for a care provider to help. Many times, the call light has actually been on, and nobody has physically come into the room. Someone might have asked, "May I help you?" from the desk, but nobody has actually addressed the need.

Responding to patients is more than responding to a call light. It is about proactively communicating and partnering with the patient and her family in her care.

You've probably heard the saying, "The best defense is a good offense." Hourly Rounding[SM] is a prime illustration of this since we are proactively addressing needs rather than responding to them. In fact, the aforementioned Studer Group study found that when an organization implements Hourly Rounding correctly, its call lights drop by 37.8 percent. And, Hourly Rounding has even been proven to save you time. When you reduce call lights, you'll be able to respond faster to the ones that *are* activated.

This tactic, coupled with a no-pass zone tactic that involves all staff in responding to a patient's needs, yields tremendous results. Patients feel they are always being assisted and cared for as soon as they need help (and sometimes before they even have to ask).

Tactic 1: Employ Hourly Rounding to Minimize Call Button Use and Impact Responsiveness

Hourly Rounding involves staff (nurses, nurse assistants, and appropriate team members) rounding on patients every hour during the day and every two hours at night. As you've already read, Hourly Rounding was the product of a study regarding call lights. It was determined that call lights occurred due to the following reasons: bathroom/bedpan assistance, IV/pump alarm, pain medication, needed a nurse, and position assistance. Of course, they can also occur because a patient can't reach her phone, book, water, and so forth. Hourly Rounding is a way to provide consistent proactive care by bundling a patient's needs into one visit and setting expectations about frequency of visits.

In order to maximize the impact of this tactic, there are specific behaviors that must be done during each round. These behaviors were developed as a result of the call light study. If we know why call lights go off, we can proactively perform certain behaviors to prevent them. Just checking in on patients every hour is helpful, but you will not see the maximum results until all eight behaviors are hardwired with all staff.

Figure 10.1

Eight Behaviors for Hourly Rounds

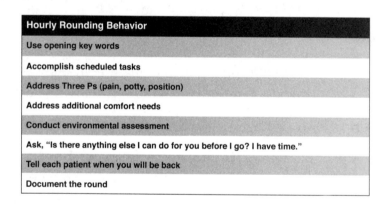

Hourly Rounding Behavior
Use opening key words
Accomplish scheduled tasks
Address Three Ps (pain, potty, position)
Address additional comfort needs
Conduct environmental assessment
Ask, "Is there anything else I can do for you before I go? I have time."
Tell each patient when you will be back
Document the round

A few tips for implementing Hourly Rounding to minimize call button use and impact responsiveness:

- **Explain Hourly Rounding.** Let the patient know that your goal is to be so responsive she doesn't even have to use the call light.
  - For example, "One of our staff members will round on you every hour during the day because we want to make sure we are meeting your needs before you have to use the call light."

  Setting the expectation of when someone will be back in to check on her helps reduce anxiety. Patients also tend to store small things they need if they know someone will come soon.

- **Share rounding hours with the patient.** Many organizations round every hour from 6 a.m. to 10 p.m., then every two hours through the night. Use key words to let the patient know why rounding occurs only every two hours at night.
  - For example, "I'll be back to check on you at midnight. Remember, at night I check on you every two hours, so that I don't disturb you as often and you can get better rest."

- **Be consistent. Round every hour without fail.** If Hourly Rounding isn't practiced every hour, patients won't be confident that someone will round and they will use their call lights. Patients need to be confident that all shifts will comply—whether it is Tuesday morning or Saturday evening.

- **Address the "Three Ps" of pain, position, and potty.** Use key words to ask about these specifically:
    - "You have been in the same position for a while. How are you feeling? Would you like to sit in a chair or at least change your position? Would you like to try going to the restroom first?"

- **Add a "P."** Some hospitals have added a fourth "P" for "pump."
    - "I am checking your pump every hour so the alarm won't go off and disturb you."

    Others have added a "P" for "personal needs" or a "P" for "patient education" to remind all staff to incorporate these important concepts in their hourly patient interactions.

- **Let patients know you are planning ahead.** If the patient has a medication schedule or therapy schedule, let her know that you are aware of it and are getting everything ready. This will put her at ease knowing you are on top of her care.
    - Use key words such as, "Your pain medication is due in an hour. Shall I get that ready and bring it with me when I come back in an hour?"

- **Prior to leaving the room, ask, "Is there anything else I can do for you before I leave?"** This is one of the best strategies to proactively meet patient needs and to eliminate call lights that interrupt work flow. It also demonstrates care, compassion, and empathy, which will impact other HCAHPS composites.

- **Manage up and remind.** Nurse leaders and other staff can manage up the patient's care providers.
  - "I see you have Julio as your nurse and Katie as your nurse aide this evening. They are some of our best employees and are so helpful. Katie is one of our best at Hourly Rounding."

  This manages up the patient's care but also creates the expectation of Hourly Rounding with the patient and staff.

- **Document Hourly Rounding.** This is important for accountability and allows verification and validation of behaviors.

- **Sign the rounding log.** Patients and their families view the logs as reassurance. When they see staff sign the log, it provides evidence that we are honoring the commitment we have made. It reduces anxiety and increases trust.
  - **Use logs as an assessment tool.** Staff members know that it's easier to round at certain times of the day than at others. Managers can review logs daily to quickly assess those hours that are most challenging.

Adjustments can be made in the rounding assignment to ensure they are completed.

- **Share results quickly.** When we see results—like reduced number of falls, steps, or call lights—we are more likely to get on board. Focus on "What's in it for me?" from your staff's perspective. For example, a reduction of 20 call lights per shift at four minutes a call light equals 80 minutes. That's one hour and 20 minutes of time returned to nurses and assistants to provide important care every shift.

Tactic 2: Create a "No-Pass Zone"

When a patient hits the call light, he is immediately watching the door for assistance to arrive. If he sees hospital staff (regardless of their role) walk past the door, he can become anxious and even frustrated. Creating a no-pass zone involves training everyone—and we mean everyone—on staff to respond to a call light.

Of course, this doesn't mean every staff member is capable of assisting a patient to the bathroom or administering pain medication. What it does mean is that every staff member can be responsive to the patient by greeting him and asking if he she can help. After all, anyone can grab a book, hand the patient a phone, the remote control, and perform a myriad of other non-clinical tasks. If the need requires a nurse, she can let the patient know assistance is on the way. Everyone, CEO included, can be held accountable to respond to a call light with, "How may I help you?" and then immediately seek the appropriate person to fulfill the request.

This sharing of responsibilities helps engage all staff members and also promotes a culture of teamwork. Of course, we would not recommend a staff member practice outside his or her comfort level, which is why all staff members are trained and understand the importance of timely response to call lights. We have partner hospitals where patients say on their surveys that, "Even the chief nursing officer answered my call light."

Following are some tips for creating a no-pass zone to improve responsiveness to call lights:

- **Make sure the nurses' station is the command center of the no-pass zone.** Here's how:
  - ○ **Assign staff to the main nurses' station.** Make sure there is someone *always* at the nurses' station to hear the call light and let the patient know that you are aware of the call light and that help is on the way. It is critical that someone physically go into the room and not just say, "May I help you?" over the intercom. This can actually be more annoying to patients, especially when a staff member answers and says that someone will be in right away, and then this doesn't happen.
  - ○ **Make sure they know how to answer the call lights.** Any staff member who may be in the nurses' station should be trained to

work the call light machine and be given key words to respond to patients.

- For example, the infection control nurse may be working at the station when the call light goes off and can respond through the intercom, "Hi, Mr. Stephenson, I see you pressed your call light...Your nurse will be with you shortly."

o **Teach them how to assess urgency.** The person at the nurses' station can help determine how acute the patient's need is from a time perspective.

- For example, if a patient requests help with the restroom say, "I see your call light is on, and someone will be in within five minutes. If you need someone immediately, I will be right down."

- **Create response time goals.** Set the expectation that all call lights need to be responded to within a certain timeframe and hold staff accountable. One Studer Group® partner has created the expectation that every call light would be answered within two minutes. Every week each nurse leader posts a list of nurses with the number of call lights over two minutes. The CNO also hosts a weekly meeting with all nurse leaders and reviews the list. For the last two quarters, the organization has been in the 99th percentile for response to call lights. And call lights are responded to not in two minutes but in one minute.

- **Train all staff in how to respond to call lights.** Teach all staff that responding to call lights is not just a nursing initiative. All staff should be trained to respond to call lights by walking into the patient's room, acknowledging the patient, either assisting (if possible) or letting the patient know the nurse is coming. Engage PT, radiology, transporters, coordinators, housekeepers, and so forth.

   On the HCAHPS survey, patients are asked how often they received help when they needed it. To achieve *always* the patient must not be kept waiting with a call light on— watching employees walk right past the door as they move on to seemingly more important things.

- **Teach staff to respond within their roles.** Training all staff means more than just asking them to not walk past a patient room when the call light is on. Training for support services and ancillary staff members should align with their roles, teaching them exactly how to respond to the patient and what assistance they can and can't provide.

- **Teach ancillary staff to conduct environmental assessments before leaving the room.** An ancillary team member can help (and in a proactive way) by surveying the room and making sure the patient has everything she needs within reach. For instance, is the remote within reach? The call light? The phone?

- **Assign a housekeeper to each unit.** Many of our partners with the highest scores have housekeepers assigned to units. This allows them to be part of the "response team" and to ensure consistency. At many organizations the housekeepers have been able to build relationships with patients and certainly have had an impact in their care.

- **Use the whiteboard to minimize call light use.** Train staff to update, review, and check the information on the whiteboard as they respond to the patient. It will hold clues as to what matters to that patient. Staff can then use that information to provide better care.
  - For example, "Mr. Caid, I see on your whiteboard that it is important for you to have a small trash bag attached to your bedside table, but I don't see one there. I will get that for you. I also want to make sure you are comfortable. Now, before I leave, is there anything else I can do to make you more comfortable?"

- **Emphasize that call lights reflect a need.** A patient may not be able to hit a call light in physical therapy or in pre-op, but he may still have a need that requires assistance. Proactively offering assistance is a sign of courtesy and respect, no matter where the patient may be located. If a patient looks like he needs assistance, do not wait to be asked; offer help. If a patient is waiting in physical therapy and can't get help, it will impact his feeling of responsiveness by staff overall.

- **Modify and verify behavior standards to account for the no-pass zone.** Behavior standards should include "Don't walk past a call light that is going off" and "Staff members are not to say, 'That room is not my patient.'" If items like these are in behavior standards, verification needs to occur to ensure that staff members are complying with them. Staff should also be trained to politely confront their colleagues who walk past call lights. They will learn to hold each other accountable for this. To make this positive and non-punitive, come up with a fun way to say, "Remember our no-pass zone."

  Many hospitals conduct actual audits on the no-pass zone. Directors or other staff are assigned to monitor hallways during random hours and note if any staff member passes a call light. Offenders can get a "passing in the no-passing zone" ticket for the first two offenses, but after that they get a verbal reprimand from their leaders. There has to be some accountability for it to be effective.

- **Set aligned goals around call lights.** To create organization-wide focus and sustained results and focus, the appropriate ancillary leaders and the nurse leaders can have a shared goal around the patients' perception of response to call lights. This is certain to build teamwork and accountability.

Most patients don't hit the call light unless they really have to. When they do, it may mean they waited as long as they could or that they tried but just couldn't do or reach something by themselves. Hourly Rounding allows us to proactively manage their needs so hopefully they won't have to wait for us to respond to call lights.

If a patient does have to hit the call light, however, a no-pass zone allows all staff to be responsive so that we can respond quickly. (In the patient's mind, he had been waiting even before he pushed the call button.)

Together, these tactics allow the entire staff to meet the patient's needs—and ensure that he gets the very best care.

Tools & Resources

Studer Group offers a variety of tools and resources that support the tactics discussed in this chapter. To access the most up-to-date offerings, please visit www.studergroup.com/HCAHPS.

To follow is a worksheet that will help you create a plan to improve patient perception of care in the "staff responsiveness" arena.

Do not underestimate the power of responsiveness. You *can* get to the point where you are not only responding quickly and efficiently to patient needs, but actually anticipating most of them and "heading them off at the pass."

When that happens, you'll reap many more benefits than just improved HCAHPS results. You'll create an organization that's known for great clinical outcomes, engaged and fulfilled employees, and, best of all, satisfied, loyal patients who receive care in a safer environment.

Responsiveness of Staff Planning Sheet

HCAHPS "TOP-BOX" PERCENTILES—December 2009 Public Reporting*

	Responsiveness of Staff Composite				
Percentile among reporting hospitals	5th	25th	50th	75th	95th
Percent of *always* responses	47	56	62	69	79

* These numbers are estimates based on historic national percentiles.

Current Responsiveness of Staff Domain Result: _____

Converted to percentile: _____

90-Day Goal: _____ Percentile: _____

Action Plan:

PAIN MANAGEMENT

A ccording to the American Pain Foundation (APF), 76.5 million Americans (1 in 4) struggle with pain without appropriate treatment. Pain is truly debilitating. In fact, the APF recommends treating pain as its own disease.

Managing patients' pain is critical. It just makes sense that when a patient's pain is under control she is comfortable, more compliant in her care, and likely to have better clinical outcomes. In fact, patients have a better perception of care based on their pain being controlled and their relationship with their care providers.

What does it mean to have pain under control? The answer depends on the patient. This section is not intended to discuss modalities of pain control. Rather, we will share how to build a relationship with each patient to improve her perception of how frequently we always helped her control her pain.

We will also share tactics that keep communication about pain front and center with the patient. We know these tactics work because our partners outperform the nation by 24 percentile points in the "pain management" composite.

Interestingly, it's not necessary to completely eradicate pain in order to change patient perception. An article in the *Journal of Pain and Symptom Management* (Gordon, Debra B., and Sandra E. Ward. "Patient Satisfaction and Pain Severity as Outcomes in Pain Management: A Longitudinal View of One Setting's Experience." *Journal of Pain and Symptom Management* 11, no. 4 (1996): 242-51.) concludes a pattern of pain relief, not pain severity, may be the critical determinant of satisfaction. Patients are more satisfied if they feel the staff cared and did everything they could to help control their pain, even if it was not completely gone.

The story below demonstrates the impact we have on patients when we work with them to manage their pain (even when they aren't sure they want help). It also shows the impact this has on patients' loved ones.

Chase was a 22-year-old male who had just been admitted following a motorcycle accident.

His doctor and I (his nurse) were in his room along with his mother. We were all concerned about his pain. However, when asked, Chase denied being in much pain. His tone said something different. He was speaking in a "macho/tough guy" fashion.

The doctor explained, "Chase, in order for us to keep your wound free of infection, your nurse and I need to 'debride and clean' it. This is basically scraping out any debris in the wound, and it's painful. I'd like to give you something for pain control prior to the procedure."

The patient rejected the medication saying, "I'm fine. I can handle it. I don't need the drugs." As he said this, the doctor noticed the patient's mom's face crinkle in worry.

The doctor decided to give it one more chance. He said, "Your mom knows you better than anyone, and the look on her face tells me you are in more pain than you are admitting. It is so hard for moms to see their sons in pain. Let's try this again, for your mom's sake. I think it's best for you to have some pain medication before we begin. Is it okay with you if we give you some?"

This resulted in a shoulder shrug and a nod of yes from the patient. It also resulted in a large smile from the mother. She was deeply relieved...and I suspect Chase was too, now that he had his mother's well-being as an "excuse" to accept the medication.

- Hannah, RN

It's true that uncontrolled pain impacts a patient's ability to heal. And as this story demonstrates, it also impacts the loved ones supporting him. When we do everything we can to control a patient's pain—and let him and his family know that we're doing it—we can make everyone feel better.

The Survey Questions

This aspect of the HCAHPS survey asks patients about their perception of the management of their pain during their hospital stay. Answers are given in frequency scale: *never, sometimes, usually,* or *always*. The percent of patients who responded "always" is publicly reported on www.hospitalcompare.hhs.gov.

Screening Question: During this hospital stay, did you need medicine for pain?

1. During this hospital stay, how often was your pain well controlled?

2. During this hospital stay, how often did the hospital staff do everything they could to help you with your pain?

In the chapters that follow, we will share the three specific tactics that positively impact the likelihood that patients will answer "always" to these two questions.

This is not a laundry list of all possible tactics. Rather, it conveys a few carefully targeted specific actions you can take to immediately impact patient perception of how well their pain is controlled.

CHAPTER ELEVEN:

CONTROL OF PAIN/ HELPFULNESS OF STAFF

THE HCAHPS QUESTION: During this hospital stay, how often was your pain well controlled?

Imagine a family member—your daughter or your mother, perhaps—lying in a hospital bed in unbearable pain. You feel helpless and just want your loved one to feel some relief. *Where is the nurse?* you wonder desperately. *Why is she in so much pain? Why don't they do something?* It doesn't take long for concern and anxiety to build to a fevered pitch. You may even become frantic and seek out staff to demand some pain relief for your loved one.

Yes, you can imagine this scenario, but you certainly don't want to experience it. And, you don't want your patients to experience it either.

We know keeping pain controllable for patients helps them heal and makes them more likely to comply with their treatment plans. And as care providers, we simply feel better when we can help our patients reach comfortable pain levels.

This question gives us insight into how well we really are controlling our patients' pain.

THE HCAHPS QUESTION: During this hospital stay, how often did the hospital staff do everything they could to help you with your pain?

As care providers we have a tremendous opportunity to make a difference in people's lives. This is especially the case with pain relief. Pain management is more than giving a Vicodin to a patient. High-performing organizations have learned that managing a patient's pain includes building a relationship with her and doing everything we can to address her specific pain needs.

Caring for the patient means caring about her pain and doing all we can to keep her pain under control. When we do this, it resonates with the patient and her family.

How do we know what it means to do "everything we can" (to paraphrase the HCAHPS question) for each patient? We have to get inside the patient's mind and understand what "everything" means to her, specifically. We need to tailor our care to her particular definition of "everything."

...AND THE TACTICS THAT MAKE "ALWAYS" RESPONSES MORE LIKELY FOR BOTH QUESTIONS

Through research with our partners nationally, we've found that the tactics used to control a patient's pain are the same ones that demonstrate staff members are doing everything they can to help manage her pain. Therefore, we've addressed these two HCAHPS questions in one chapter.

To achieve such great results under this composite, our partners have used Individualized Patient Care (IPC) to understand what "controlled pain" is to each patient and what it means to each patient to do everything possible to help her achieve it. IPC is a communication methodology that enables us to connect and communicate with patients *as individuals* as we partner to manage their pain.

We've found Hourly Rounding^SM to be the best tactic to communicate with patients about pain and to take steps to proactively manage it.

Finally, to keep the management of pain as a constant, many partners have implemented the pain poster. It provides a visual reminder of the patient's pain expectations along with important pain management information.

The end result? Patients get that all-important pattern of pain relief and a consistent focus on pain management and communication...and they *always* feel staff helped control their pain.

Tactic 1: Use Individualized Patient Care to Manage Patient Perception of Pain

When our partners use Individualized Patient Care, they are finding out what's important to the patient: from the patient's perspective, what will reduce her anxiety and demonstrate their sensitivity to her concerns. Managing pain is usually high on the list.

IPC is about learning from the patient and aligning their care (and especially their words) accordingly: "Tell me what pain control means to you...Tell me what pain well-controlled means to you...Tell me what a 5 on the pain scale looks like to you...Tell me what it means to you to have staff do everything to help you...Tell me what you expect. Do you have any questions?"

This approach allows our partners to find out patients' expectations regarding pain upfront so there will be no "unmet or unrealistic expectations" later. It alleviates the gaps in perception of pain management. In other words, if your staff and patient are on the same page from the beginning regarding what "controlled pain" looks like— or if staff members are able to help her manage her expectations—it's easier to positively impact the patient's perception of this issue.

Once the patient feels like you haven't controlled her pain, it may be too late to change her perception. Or worse, she may feel that you don't really care about helping her control her pain.

Here are a few tips for implementing IPC to impact the "staff doing everything they can to control pain management" perception:

- **Ask questions about pain.** Ask probing questions to gain a good understanding of what the patient expects in terms of controlling pain. Ask questions like: "What do you consider manageable pain?" "What is tolerable?" "What do you expect in terms of pain management?" "What has worked for you in the past?"

- **Use the pain scale.** Pain assessment is very important. The pain scale can be used to manage expectations and create agreement. The conversation could go something like this: "Tell me where you are on the pain scale right now...If we could get your pain down to a 3, would that be a good goal to work toward?...I'm going to circle where your pain is on the board and then circle where your pain goal is. As I visit you hourly, we'll talk about your pain and update the pain scale."

  The goal is for the pain level and pain goal to align and allow the nurse to get a win. "Wonderful, when I began my shift, your pain was at a 7 and now it is at a 3. That was the goal you set."

- **Manage patients' pain expectations.** It is often not feasible for patients to have no pain. Sometimes patients *will* feel pain and it's important to acknowledge that fact.

○ **Use key words.** Address expectations with key words such as:

- "We are going to do the best job we can to manage your pain as safely as possible. Your safety is our number one priority, and if the medicine Dr. Mark ordered isn't working, he asked us to call and let him know. For now, I am going to give you as much as I can, as fast as I can, and as safely as I can to control your pain the best I can. We may not get you pain-free but we are going to do the best we can."

○ **Seek agreement on pain levels.** Discuss what controlling pain looks like (i.e., what's a tolerable or acceptable pain level for the patient).

- "We want to make you comfortable, but there may be some discomfort inherent with your condition. We'll do all we can to keep your pain manageable for you."

○ **Be sensitive to the patient's desire for more pain medication.** Help her understand the effects of too much medication.

- "Too much of this pain medication won't allow you to get up and gain strength, thereby prolonging your healing time."

Explaining this connects the dots for the patient, and she will be more compliant.

- **Seek alternatives to pain medicine.** In addition to pain medication, check to see if the patient is open to alternatives beyond additional pain medicine. Not all pain management is in the form of medication. There are other tactics to use: relaxation, soft music, deep breathing, turning off lights, repositioning, cool compresses, warm compresses, and simply closing the door to allow the patient to rest.

  Ask, "When you are home, how do you get comfortable?" This question may trigger the patient to remember something she's done at home that helped her manage pain.

- **Reposition the patient.** We reposition patients for many reasons and one of them is pain management. Use words to explain what you are doing.
  - "Let's try a new position that may alleviate your pain a bit." Or, "Let's try changing a few things to see how this impacts your progress. I'm going to elevate your feet a bit." Or, "Let's shift you to this side."

- **Address pain at shift change.** The patient's expectations should be readdressed as the new nurse comes on staff.
  - For example, the new nurse says, "Let's talk about your plan of care for my shift. Tell me about your pain level."

  If you are doing Bedside Shift Report^{SM}, this is an excellent time to review when the last pain medication was given and how the patient tolerated it. The reassessment can be done and documented as well.

- **Coordinate pain medication with ancillary procedures.** Ensure that the patient's pain medication schedule is coordinated with other activities (radiology, cardiology, physical therapy, and so forth).
  - ○ **Medication schedule.** The nurse can be aware of timing for medications and work with ancillary to ensure that pain medication administration is not impacted by the patient being away from her room.
  - ○ **Ancillary involvement in pain management.** Pain control and timing of pain medications should be taken into account by all departments interacting with patients. If you know a patient is going to physical therapy for the first time, ensure that she is pre-medicated appropriately.

- **Inquire about pain during post-visit calls.** A phone call after the patient has left the hospital to check on how she is doing and to ask about her pain is a tremendous demonstration of care and concern.

Tactic 2: Conduct Hourly Rounding to Consistently Address Pain

Hourly Rounding is more than just "checking in" on the patient. It is about combining tasks and being proactive in his care. When we address the patient's pain every hour, it allows us to keep a tight handle on his pain so it doesn't get out of control.

To the patient, these frequent visits demonstrate that we care. And if every time we check on him, we ask about his pain and what we can do to manage it, we're telling the patient, "We want to do everything we can to control your pain and help you be comfortable." It makes a difference in the eyes of the patient and his family.

Below are some tips:

- **Address pain during each Hourly Round.** Every time the nurse goes into the patient's room, she can address pain and/or reassess the pain level following intervention to determine effectiveness. She can say, "Tell me how you are doing with your pain. This is where you said you wanted to be; tell me where you are now."
  - ○ **Use key words.**
    - For example, you might say: "I want to do everything I can to make you as comfortable as possible. Keeping your pain managed is important. Tell me about your pain right now."

    The phrase "everything I can" is key to the patient's understanding the staff's goal of helping him with pain. Just be careful not to word questions exactly as they appear in the HCAHPS survey or to phrase key words in an unnatural way.
  - ○ **Alleviate anxiety.** Let the patient know that you will be checking on his pain every hour,

but that you won't disturb him when he is resting. When a patient trusts that you will be back and checking on him regularly, he tends to rest better and have less anxiety.

- **Tell the patient when his next dose of pain medication is coming.** This will allow him to mentally prepare for that length of time.
  - ○ "I gave you a dose three hours ago, and your next dose is in about an hour. Would you like me to prepare and bring it in with me when it is due?"

- **Use the whiteboard.** With his permission, write the next time the patient can have pain medication on the whiteboard, so other staff, physicians, and even family can see the schedule. If the patient is experiencing a high level of pain, trend the pain level on the whiteboard each hour. It can demonstrate movement in the right direction when the patient sees his pain level is continuing to trend down.

- **Encourage two-way conversation about pain.** The hourly visit should not feel rushed or scripted. Rather it can be used as an opportunity to truly demonstrate empathy and connect with the patient. If you are going to ask about his pain, take time to establish eye contact and pay attention to the answer. Assess his non-verbal cues as he tells you about his pain.

- **For new pain medications, provide a complete explanation.** If new medications are being given at that hour's visit, explain them thoroughly, addressing all the components of each including side effects. (See Communication of Medication composite for review.)

- **Show the win.** Look for opportunities to share improvement with the patient.
  - "Last time you needed 6 mg of medication after six hours; now you need only 3 mg for six hours. We are making progress."

Tactic 3: Pain Poster

The pain poster is just that: a poster that holds important patient pain information.

The poster is a visual reminder for the patient, family, and staff. It reduces the worry and anxiety over when the patient can have her next dose of pain medication. It alleviates the likelihood of the patient saying, "I'm starting to feel pain. I wonder when my next pain dose is due." When the patient is able to see when she will receive another dose, she can mentally prepare herself and manage her pain.

Figure 11.1

Pain Poster

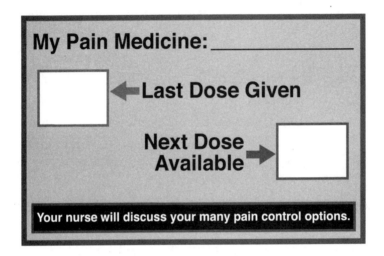

It's also a terrific family communicator. When family members walk in and the patient says she's in pain, the poster provides reassurance. It prevents the family from thinking the patient's pain hasn't been managed. They can instead support the patient by saying, "It looks like you have to wait only half an hour for more pain medication. Can you make it another half hour?"

Without exception, this poster has impacted the patient's perception of care. One partner launched this in an orthopedic unit and moved the Pain Management composite from the 66th percentile to the 99th percentile in one quarter. The organization quickly launched it hospital-wide and achieved similar results.

The poster gives the nurse the opportunity to move from communicating about pain medication to communicating about medications in general. It opens up conversations about dosing and side effects.

The pain poster helps the nurse leader to validate that appropriate tactics have been implemented. It also sets the nurse up to know that he or she is being held accountable to explain the medicines.

Finally, the pain poster will also impact the Communication of Medication composite.

Here are some tips to help you implement the pain poster:

- **Remember: location, location, location.** The poster needs to be in a spot that the patient, the family, and the hospital staff can easily see. It should be hung in the same location in every room so staff know exactly where to look.

- **Share the *why*.** Let the patient and her family know the poster was developed to keep them informed about her pain medication. It keeps everyone on the same page in terms of pain management.

- **Use with the pain scale to manage progress.** Ask the patient, "So how's your pain on a scale of 1-10?" The patient may say it's a 4. The nurse may remember or may look at the chart and say, "So your medication is working because last time you said it was a 9. We gave this only 20 minutes ago and now it's down to a 4. I'm glad that we're controlling it."

- **Reward staff.** As nurse leaders round on patients and see the pain poster filled in and the patients feeling like their pain management is a priority, they can go back to staff and immediately recognize them for the difference they are making.

Note that some partners have incorporated the key elements of the pain poster onto their whiteboards rather than creating a separate poster. Either way works. The important part is to have a visual reminder for patients that you are doing everything you can to manage their pain.

All three of these tactics—IPC, Hourly Rounding, and the pain poster—show patients that you care about keeping them as comfortable as possible. Together, they are sure to impact patients' perception of the care you provide. And best of all, they'll help patients heal and enjoy better clinical outcomes.

Tools & Resources

Studer Group offers a variety of tools and resources that support the tactics discussed in this chapter. To access the most up-to-date offerings, please visit www.studergroup.com/HCAHPS.

To follow is a worksheet that will help you create a plan to improve patient perception of care in the "pain management" arena.

One of the noblest goals of medicine is to alleviate human suffering. That's what you're doing when you hardwire these pain management tactics. They're about much, much more than HCAHPS results. As you roll out and implement these tactics, help staff members connect back to this truth—you'll find more success and help everyone who works at your organization remember their sense of purpose.

Pain Management Planning Sheet

HCAHPS "TOP-BOX" PERCENTILES—December 2009 Public Reporting*

	Pain Management Composite				
Percentile among reporting hospitals	5th	25th	50th	75th	95th
Percent of *always* responses	58	65	68	72	78

* These numbers are estimates based on historic national percentiles.

Current Pain Management Domain Result: _____

Converted to percentile: _____

90-Day Goal: _____ Percentile: _____

Action Plan:

Communication of Medications

Nearly 1 in every 5 patients experiences an adverse event after being discharged from the hospital. And according to the *Annals of Internal Medicine*, 66 percent of these events are medication-related. When we don't communicate and communicate often with all of the necessary details about a medication and its side effects, we are putting our patients in danger.

Here are a couple more disturbing statistics:

- Based on a Mayo Clinic study, we know that 72 percent of patients who are discharged from the hospital are not able to recite their own medication list. (O'Leary, Kevin J., et al. "Hospitalized Patients' Understanding of Their Plan of Care." *Mayo Clinic Proceedings* 85, no. 1 (2010): 47-52.)

- According to the Institute of Medicine, more than 1.5 million Americans are injured each year from medicine errors in healthcare facilities. This results in upward of $3.5 billion in extra medical costs. ("Medication Errors Injure 1.5 Million People and Cost Billions of Dollars Annually; Report Offers Comprehensive Strategies for Reducing Drug-Related Mistakes." *Office of News and Public Information. Institute of Medicine. National Academies.* 20 July 2006. <http://www8.nationalacademies.org/onpinews/newsitem.aspx?RecordID=11623> (27 July 2010).)

It's clear that there is much work to be done in communicating with patients regarding their medications. The good news? When organizations implement the three tactics described in the following chapter, patients' perception that they are being communicated with about their medications will rise. We know because our partners perform on average 17 percentile points higher than the nation on the HCAHPS Communication of Medications composite.

Improving our communication in this critical area is about *always* letting patients and their families know what medications have been prescribed and why. It is about *always* sharing with patients the side effects that may impact them. It is about *always* conveying the *why* to patients so they are more likely to comply with treatments and get better outcomes. This is all information patients need to know—not just to raise HCAHPS scores but to do everything we possibly can to ensure their safety and well-being.

The following story, which relays the experience of a quality assurance nurse, demonstrates why communicating about medications is the absolute right thing to do for the patient.

During quality checks on a hospital unit, I asked if we could walk into a nearby patient's room in order to round. The nurses protested. They said, in essence, that we shouldn't go into that particular patient's room because "he's not very nice."

Of course, the minute I heard this, my mind was made up—I was absolutely going in that room. Again, the nurses expressed their hesitation. They said, "He's crabby, he's mean, and he doesn't like us." Naturally, this only strengthened my resolve.

I went into the patient's room, introduced myself, and asked, "How has your stay been?"

"It's been pretty good at this hospital, but I don't think they like me very much," the patient replied.

"Why is that?" I asked.

"Because every time they bring me medication, I ask them exactly what it is and what it's for. I kind of give them the third degree."

"I wish every patient we have in the hospital would exercise that right," I replied.

"Well, I appreciate that," he said. "You see, I'm allergic to Hydrocodone. Three years ago, I was at the hospital and I had on my arm bracelet—no one checked it. They gave me medicine without telling me what it was for. It turned out to have Hydrocodone in it. Anyway, I had an allergic reaction. I about stopped breathing and ended up in the ICU.

"If I had been asking and had they been doing their jobs, I wouldn't have had that happen," he continued. "So now I ask them every time, 'What are you bringing me? What is it for? What is it

going to do?' I get really nervous now. I don't ever want to be in that situation again."

- Paul, Quality Assurance Nurse

It turned out this "crabby" man wasn't crabby at all. He was nervous and scared. He needed better communication from hospital staff regarding the medication they were giving him. That's what all patients need from all hospital staff. When we provide it, we gain their understanding and their partnership in the care we are providing.

The Survey Questions

This aspect of the HCAHPS survey asks patients about their perception of communication of medications during their hospital stay. Answers are given in frequency scale: *never, sometimes, usually,* or *always.* The percent of patients who respond "always" is publicly reported on www. hospitalcompare.hhs.gov.

Screening Question: During this hospital stay, were you given any medicine that you had not taken before?

1. Before giving you any new medicine, how often did hospital staff tell you what the medicine was for?

2. Before giving you any new medicine, how often did hospital staff describe possible side effects in a way you could understand?

In the chapter that follows, we will share the three specific tactics that positively impact the likelihood that patients will answer "always" to two of the above questions. (The first question is a screening question, and patients will not answer the following questions if they answer "no" to the screening question.)

This is not a laundry list of all possible tactics. Rather, it conveys a few carefully targeted specific actions you can take to immediately impact patient perception of how well you communicated with them regarding medications.

IMPORTANT NOTE: The tactics in this section do *not* replace medication reconciliation work with patients or education for nursing staff or multi-disciplinary teams working to improve this process. However, we have found that they go a long way toward driving outcomes, especially in hospitals that are already working hard on The Joint Commission, national patient safely goals, and multi-disciplinary medication reconciliation teams.

CHAPTER TWELVE:

EXPLANATION REGARDING MEDICATIONS AND SIDE EFFECTS

THE HCAHPS QUESTION: Before giving you any new medicine, how often did hospital staff tell you what the medicine was for?

We know it is no longer acceptable to walk into a patient's room, hand him a pill and a little cup of water, and ask him to take the medicine…yet it happens. Evidence (and common sense) tells us that when patients are involved in and understand their treatment plan, they are more likely to comply and their outcomes are more likely to be better. This is particularly important when it comes to what a medication is for and why it is important that the patient take it as prescribed.

As healthcare professionals we have a real opportunity to communicate these basic facts. A study published in the *Archives of Internal Medicine* found that 66 percent of patients surveyed did not know the duration of treatment of their medication. (Hays, Ron D., et al. "Physician

Communication When Prescribing New Medications."
Archives of Internal Medicine 166, no. 17 (2006): 1855-62.)

This question gives us a valuable opportunity to gauge whether we are always letting patients know they are being given a new medication, what that medication is for, and what to expect from it.

THE HCAHPS QUESTION: Before giving you any new medicine, how often did hospital staff describe possible side effects in a way you could understand?

Being in the hospital causes anxiety. New medications cause anxiety. Worrying how a medication will impact you definitely causes anxiety. Consider the results of a recent study showing that only 35 percent of patients knew the side effects of their medication and you'll realize we have the power to reduce that anxiety—just by communicating. (Hays, Ron D., et al. "Physician Communication When Prescribing New Medications." *Archives of Internal Medicine* 166, no. 17 (2006): 1855-62.)

It is vital that patients understand what side effects are associated with the medications they have been prescribed. We don't want patients to worry and wonder with thoughts like, *My heart is racing; am I having a heart attack?* Or, *I am nauseated. What if I can't keep this medication down?* They should also know what to do if they experience a side effect.

One thing's for sure: The worry and anxiety caused by not knowing enough about the side effects of medication will not help the patient heal. In fact, studies show that having too little information can cause the patient to not cooperate with treatment and medication regimens and can lead to poor clinical outcomes.

...AND THE TACTICS THAT MAKE "ALWAYS" RESPONSES MORE LIKELY (FOR BOTH QUESTIONS)

Through research we at Studer Group® have built the components of a proper explanation of medications. These components are centered on what patients and their family members need and want to know about the medications in order to put them at ease and help them become willing partners in their treatment. One of these components focuses on side effects.

We've found that we use the exact same tactics to help our partners be successful with communicating about patient medications in general and communicating about side effects. Therefore, we've addressed these two HCAHPS questions in one chapter. When you implement these three tactics and focus on sharing all the components of medication, patients will perceive their care to be better...and it will be.

One of these tactics is Key Words at Key Times, a communication style our partners use to improve the quality of information provided and ensure a two-way dialogue between individuals. Focusing on key words ensures that patients are educated about their new medications and that this teaching is reinforced by all appropriate staff members. With each dose given, a nurse can reinforce education and encourage communication with a patient, thus reinforcing the patient's knowledge of his medication.

The Bedside Shift Report[SM] is another tactic our partners use to communicate with patients regarding medication. During this three-way conversation between the outgoing nurse, the oncoming nurse, and the patient, it is relatively easy to add key words around medications. This is another example of how our high-performing partners integrate the HCAHPS questions into their care delivery and hardwire these "handoffs."

Finally, post-visit or discharge phone calls are used to check in on the patient and reinforce his medication needs and possible side effects. They allow the nurse to ensure the patient had a safe transition home.

Together, these three tactics provide a high level of communication about medications to the patient—placing him at ease, engaging him as a partner in his care, and, in the end, helping him enjoy better clinical outcomes.

Tactic 1: Use Key Words to Ensure Two-Way Dialogue about Medications

Communicating about medications with the patient means sharing the right information frequently. For all of us, awareness and learning require repetition. In fact, it's said that the average adult needs to be exposed to new information at least three times in order to commit it to memory. And in a hospital situation when patients and their families are often faced with pain and uncertainty, it is even more important to take the time to clearly explain medications and side effects in a meaningful way.

Key Words at Key Times ensure we have effectively communicated the *what* and the *why* to patients. This is especially critical when giving a patient a new medication that he will be required to manage himself when he goes home in three days. Patients need to know *what* they are taking, and they need to know *why* they are taking it.

The tactic affords us an opportunity to ensure we are proactively assessing a patient's knowledge about his medications, assessing for gaps in his knowledge about side effects of medications or drug interactions, and identifying any barriers to his compliance with his medication treatment plan. A culture of *always* around medication information is critical for patient compliance and quality outcomes.

Using key words represents an important strategy to ensure all staff members who interact with patients about medications are communicating in an effective and efficient manner. From the physician who orders a new prescription, to the nurse who administers a daily medication, to the respiratory therapist who uses medications in her respiratory treatments, to the case manager who educates a patient family about home care—all staff can use key words to ensure we have shared information about all medications and their common side effects. When all staff members reinforce this critical element of safe, patient-centered care, we will truly impact patient outcomes in a positive manner.

This certainly includes readmissions to the hospital. One study funded by the Agency for Healthcare Research and Quality (AHRQ) showed that patients who have a clear understanding of their after-hospital care instructions, including how to take their medicines, are 30 percent less likely to be readmitted or visit the Emergency Department than those who lack this information. The study found that total costs were an average of $412 lower for the patients who received complete information than for those who did not. (Anthony, David, et al. "A Reengineered Hospital Discharge Program to Decrease Rehospitalization: A Randomized Trial." *Annals of Internal Medicine* 150, no. 3 (2009): 178-87.)

Educating patients about their home care, medications, and follow-up appointments makes good financial sense, and it is just good medicine.

Here are some tips to help you implement Key Words at Key Times—and to emphasize communication of medicines and their side effects:

- **Hardwire an explanation of every medication with every dosage given.** When "accomplishing scheduled tasks of medication administration"—a key behavior of Hourly Rounding[SM]—talk about medications with the patient. This communication should be documented and hardwired in the same way that you hardwire asking the patient about his pain level. (Tip: To help hardwire, add it to the Hourly Rounding Log.)

- **Encourage two-way communication.** Take
the time to pause as you move through the medication explanation. Give the patient a chance to let the
information soak in and also to ask you any questions. This should be more of a conversation than
a lecture, so use patient-friendly terminology. Stick
to sixth-grade language. If you use words, phrases,
terms, and acronyms not understood by the patient,
it might discourage two-way dialogue because the
patient may be too embarrassed to say he doesn't
know what you are talking about.

- **When explaining a medication, always share
six critical components.** Following is all the
information a patient needs to know in order to
partner in his care—and to be more likely to comply
with the medication instructions.
    - **Name of the medication:** Use the name
    of the medication as ordered. Doctors may
    order generic or brand name medication, so
    don't confuse patients by calling it something
    else. Connect the dots if there is a common
    name for it. For example, Zocor is a brand
    name for a drug that treats cholesterol and
    triglycerides. The generic name is Simvasta-
    tin. If a patient takes "Zocor" at home but
    is taking "Simvastatin" in the hospital, he
    might be confused. It may impress the patient
    to hear these long names but he likely won't
    be able to commit it to memory and it could
    raise anxiety. Knowing the exact name allows

him to tell other care providers (and it could be at another hospital or an outpatient clinic) the medications he is on. This could prevent two incompatible drugs being prescribed. Confusion about medication names can be a big problem. We actually heard about one patient who was on three medications that all treated the same condition due to confusion between brand name and generic drugs prescribed by multiple care providers.

○ **Purpose of the medication:** When patients do not comprehend all aspects of their conditions or the importance of taking a specific medication, they are less likely to adhere to the treatment plan. (Harmon, G., M. Krousel-Wood, and J. Lefante. "Overcoming Barriers: the Role of Providers in Improving Patient Adherence to Antihypertensive Medications." *Current Opinion in Cardiology* 21, no. 4 (2006) 310-15.) Share with the patient why *this medication* has been selected and how it will make him heal or be healthier.

○ **Duration of the medication:** Let the patient know how long he should anticipate taking the medication. Is it just for this hospital stay? Will he need to take it upon discharge? Is it a lifelong medication? Reinforce what the physician has told him about the medication and assess patient readiness to learn.

- ○ **When the medication will take effect:** If relevant, share the length of time the patient should expect to wait before feeling the effects. Some medications can make a patient very uncomfortable. This will help him plan his day. For example, he can ask grandchildren to visit earlier in the day before the medicine takes effect.

- ○ **Dosage:** Let the patient know the amount of medication he will be taking. It can also reduce anxiety to let him know what to do if a dose is missed or how strict the timing requirements are. When we tell a patient to take a medication every six hours, do we really mean he is to set his clock and wake up in the middle of the night to take it?

- ○ **Side effects:** Let the patient know of any potential side effects. Make sure to use the words "side effects." When we say, "Let me know if you have any nausea," the patient might not connect the dots that this is a common side effect of this medication.

  - Explain common side effects: Sometimes medications have side effects that are irritating or can cause some discomfort but are manageable considering the alternative (i.e., the disease not being treated). Let the patient know that these common side effects are okay as long as he finds them manageable, and they can also be treated to make him more comfortable.

- Explain side effects to watch out for: If side effects are harmful or dangerous, explain, "This medication is very effective at treating the specific infection that you have. However, a small percentage of patients who take it develop a rash. Although we will be in every hour to check on you, if you notice this, please let one of us know immediately. If this occurs, we would want to change the medication before you develop other symptoms of an allergic reaction." Validate the patient's understanding by asking him to tell you the 1-2 most common side effects of the medication(s) you have just discussed.

- Let him know there are alternatives: Explain to the patient that there are alternative medications, so he is aware that if he gets a side effect he can't handle, he has options. Patients should be encouraged to ask their physicians if there are any alternatives to the medication if the side effects should turn out to be unmanageable.

- Mention drug-on-drug and drug-on-food interactions: Let the patient know if there are any other medications that he should watch out for. Also, share if there are any food restrictions due to potential reaction with the medication, or if it is necessary to take a specific medication with food. For example, some antibiotics should not be taken with milk, so the patient should be aware of this if he is taking a medication at meal time.

- **Ask for the patient's compliance.** Make sure he has the information he needs to agree to comply with the medication requirements. When a patient agrees, he is much more likely to comply with the treatment plan.
  - Ask, "Is there anything that might prevent you from taking this medication when you go home?"

- **Use AIDET℠ to educate about medications.**
  - A = Acknowledge. "Mr. Perdue, I have the new medication your doctor ordered for your blood pressure."
  - I = Introduce. "Since it is new to you, I want to take some time to tell you about it—why you are taking it and some side effects to watch out for. Is now a good time? You are taking

(name of medication) and it will help lower your blood pressure."

- D = Duration. "You will take it just once a day. You will need to remain on this medication through your follow-up appointment in two weeks."
- E = Explanation. "Most people don't have any trouble with this medication but some of the more common side effects we have seen are dizziness and cough. I have printed out this information about your new medication for you to read and review. I am going to highlight two things on this page for you to review because it is important you understand your medication when you go home. We will review it again before you are discharged too. It is important you know what the medication is, why you are taking it, and what the common side effects are. Let's go over it one more time."
- T = Thank you. "Thank you for paying such close attention. It is important you understand your medications so you can heal faster and care for yourself when you go home. Let me know if you have any questions after you read through this."

- **Reinforce education about medications regularly.** Check back regularly with the patient to ensure that he has absorbed what he needs to know about medication.

    - You can ask open-ended questions during Hourly Rounding such as, "Why do we have you on fall precautions?" Or, "We talked about side effects of the medication earlier—can you tell me what they were?" "Tell me how you think you're handling the new medication you started?" "Do you remember the name of the medication we talked about earlier?"

- **Use the whiteboard to communicate with other staff about medication education.** This will reinforce the information shared and also trigger other staff members to ask pertinent questions— "How is your new medication? Tell me about the side effects; are you experiencing any?"—when they visit the patient.

- **Be consistent.** Key words work best when all staff members use consistent messaging to maximize the impact of incorporating communication regarding medication. This means it needs to happen at least 90 percent of the time.

- **Validate and verify with nurse leader rounding.** Use nurse leader rounding to ensure education about medications and their common side effects happens.

- ○ The nurse leader can say to the patient: "One of my goals as a nurse leader is to make sure that our nurses are teaching you about your medicines and any possible side effects. What did you learn from your nurse today? How often did she discuss your medications and possible side effects?"

Tactic 2: Reinforce Medication Education into the Bedside Shift Report

Patients look to their nurses for their hour-to-hour communication and care. As the nurse provides care throughout his shift, a deepening of the relationship occurs. The nurse knows the medications the patient is on, how she is responding to the medications, and how she feels.

As one nurse leaves and a new nurse comes on, patient anxiety is high. The patient is left wondering, *Will the new nurse be as good? Will he understand what is happening with me? Will he know about my reaction to that medication? Will he know when my next dose is needed?* She may be worried that the new nurse doesn't have all of the information needed to care for her.

The Bedside Shift Report can reassure her on all these fronts. This tactic is the ultimate in transition of care. It gains the patient's confidence, involves her in her own care, and serves as another teaching opportunity for her. By taking a report that has to happen regardless and building in patient involvement, we maximize our efforts.

Conveying the information this way has many benefits. The patient understands her care and her new medications. She is reassured because she plays an active role in the handoff of her care. She doesn't have to worry whether the new nurse knows what medications she is on or which side effects could occur. In addition, the Bedside Shift Report is an opportunity for the outgoing nurse to bring the oncoming nurse up to speed and to verify medication information. It is okay—indeed, even better—to ask the patient to let her new nurse know what medications she is on and what the side effects are. (The more she repeats this information, the better she'll come to know it.)

A few tips:

- **Review the printed list of medications.**
  During each Bedside Shift Report, review medications with the patient and the new nurse. This will ensure all are on the same page. The patient should play an active role. Ask her to share any new medications that have been prescribed during that shift as well as side effects and other important information.
    - Printed list of medications: Give a sheet with all the medications listed together to the patient. This becomes a useful tool even when she leaves the hospital.

- **Highlight medication instructions...literally.**
  On the medication sheet that is given to the patient,
  highlight (or have her highlight) the salient information. This will provide the patient with the key
  information she needs to know and where to look to
  refresh her memory. Have her highlight the name of
  the medication, the purpose of the medication, and
  three common side effects.

- **Engage the patient in the conversation.**
  During bedside reporting, the patient can be asked
  to tell the oncoming nurse about any new medications and what she learned about side effects.
    - "Mrs. Jones, you had a new medication for
      the first time today. Can you tell John what
      you are taking the medicine for and the side
      effects you should look out for?"
    - "Mrs. Jones, John is going to be your nurse
      tonight, and I have told him about your new
      medications. Can you tell him what you
      learned about that medicine today?"

- **Re-explain the medication as a team.** At shift
  change the outgoing nurse and the patient should
  go through the explanation of the medication together with the oncoming nurse. Having the patient
  involved helps her better understand and remember
  the medication. It also gives the nurse coming on a
  better sense of the patient's concerns and ability to
  remember the important information.

Tactic 3: Make Post-Visit Calls and Include Medication Information

Rarely does anyone have a patient who is not in a hurry to be discharged from the hospital. As the patient is packing (or is already all packed) and just waiting for approval, the nurse takes him through everything he needs to do once he gets home. Unfortunately, much of this information is not retained...likely because the patient can think only about getting out of the hospital.

Remember that statistic we cited at the beginning of this chapter? A Mayo Clinic study found that 72 percent of patients who are discharged from the hospital are not able to recite their own medication list. It is not surprising, therefore, that 1 in every 5 patients has an adverse event post-discharge.

Post-visit or discharge phone calls offer us the opportunity to extend the care we provide outside the hospital. They allow us to check in with patients and hear how they are doing and whether they have all of the information they need regarding their medications.

A few tips:

- **Check on the medication.** Make sure the patient was able to get the prescription filled and that he has access to the medication. Re-emphasize the importance and purpose of the medication to encourage compliance.
    - Ask, "Were you able to get your prescription filled?"

- **Link back.** Refer back to communication regarding medication in the hospital. This may help him remember, and it will demonstrate consistency of care.
    - Ask, "Remember when your nurses would change shift and review your medications?"

- **Use key words that align with explanation of medication.** Build key words around the steps used to explain medications.
    - Say, "Now that you are home, what medications are you taking? What are those medications for? What side effects are you watching out for?"

- **Have the primary nurses call.** These calls save lives regardless of who makes the calls. But when a nurse who cared for the patient makes the call, the impact is greater for the patient and for the nurse. The call builds on the relationship they established while the patient was in the hospital.

- **Help staff members connect these calls back to purpose.** In our national lab of partner hospitals, we consistently hear how these calls save lives. These are not a "nice to do" —they are a "must do" if we want to ensure a safe transition home. When a nurse hears the gratitude in a patient's voice for her taking the time to make a call and check on his safety, the nurse understands she is truly making a difference in the patient's life. And in the rare instance she can save a life because of a phone call, she will be a lifelong zealous supporter of post-visit calls.

Medications are powerful forces for healing, but used improperly they can cause harm. These three tactics—Key Words at Key Times, Bedside Shift Report, and Post-Visit Phone Calls—will help staff members ensure that patients maximize the beneficial properties of medications and minimize the risks.

Tools & Resources

Studer Group offers a variety of tools and resources that support the tactics discussed in this chapter. To access the most up-to-date offerings, please visit www.studergroup.com/HCAHPS.

To follow is a worksheet that will help you create a plan to improve patient perception of care in the "communication of medications" arena.

We give medications in order to help patients heal. What we tell them about those medications—as well as how often we tell them and which words we use—is critical to ensuring that these intentions are met. The tactics you've just learned are about far more than achieving higher HCAHPS results. They're about restoring good health and saving lives—and nothing we do is more important than that.

Communication of Medications Planning Sheet

HCAHPS "TOP-BOX" PERCENTILES—December 2009 Public Reporting*

	Communication of Medications Composite				
Percentile among reporting hospitals	5th	25th	50th	75th	95th
Percent of *always* responses	48	55	58	63	71

* These numbers are estimates based on historic national percentiles.

Current Communication of Medications Domain Result: _____

Converted to percentile: _____

90-Day Goal: _____ Percentile: _____

Action Plan:

DISCHARGE INFORMATION

According to the *Annals of Internal Medicine*, nearly 1 in 5 patients experience an adverse event upon leaving the hospital. Why? In part it's because at discharge the patient is often so focused on leaving she may not retain the information that can keep her safe. For that reason, discharge really needs to start at admission. (Bates, D. W., et al. "The Incidence and Severity of Adverse Events Affecting Patients after Discharge from the Hospital." *Annals of Internal Medicine* 138, no. 3 (2003): 161-67.) Remember, repetition leads to retention. It's the best way to ensure that our end goal is met—a safe transition home for the patient (and avoided readmission).

According to IHI, a "Medicare Payment Advisory Commission (MedPAC) Medicare data analysis found that $12 billion in readmission costs were potentially preventable. In addition, there is evidence documenting the high rates of readmissions for patients with certain conditions such as congestive heart failure (CHF). Among the populations studied, CHF 30-day readmission rates are particularly high at approximately 20 to 24 percent." Not only are these readmissions disruptive to the patient and family, in the very near future, the hospital will no longer be reimbursed for them.

Planning for discharge upon admission allows us to share, repeat, and ensure retention of important information throughout the patient's stay. It allows us to provide a continuum of care by connecting the information staff members provide during the hospital stay to the patient's care at home. It also keeps the patient thinking about the next phase of her care—and that's exactly what it is. When the patient leaves the hospital, she isn't leaving our care; it's just that the responsibility for managing the details shifts to her and her home caregivers. This is a tremendous responsibility and one that is critical to excellent outcomes and our goal of reducing costly readmissions.

The responses to the two HCAHPS questions in the Discharge Information composite allow a hospital to see how well it's helping patients make the transition between inpatient care and home care. When analyzing our national lab of hospitals, we find that Studer Group® partners perform more than 10 percentile points above the national average in this composite. By following the tactics they use, you can improve your scores in this area, too.

When you start sharing discharge information at admission, you allow time for the patient to begin discussing medications, diet, dressing changing, or other instructions she'll need to know once she goes home. What's more, thinking about going home is a healthy psychological focus for the patient—it gives her something positive to work toward. It also includes her (and her family) in the care plan and helps manage expectations regarding length of stay.

When you truly hardwire the processes for sharing this information with patients early on, the conversation that takes place on the day of discharge is essentially a recap and a clarification. If it's done effectively, there should be very little that is "new" to a patient regarding her home care plan.

None of this is meant to downplay final discharge instructions. While education throughout the patient's stay may prepare her for managing her own care, her perception of the instructions she gets at the time of discharge will still make the greatest impact on how she feels when she leaves the hospital. We still need to ask the pertinent questions one final time: *Is the patient confident in what medications she needs? Does she know why she is taking the medication and does she know the most important side effects to look for? Does she have numbers to call with questions? Does she know how and when to make a follow-up appointment?*

When we prepare the patient and her family for discharge from the moment she is admitted until the time she leaves the hospital, her confidence and compliance will increase.

Post-visit phone calls also help reinforce discharge instructions. We hear stories all the time like the one below that show their value.

Our unit had just implemented post-visit calls, and we were listening to Dwight, our nurse leader, make some calls. As he called patients, he had the discharge instructions, including the medication list, in front of him.

One woman the nurse leader called was to go home on Lovinox, an important medication that requires the patient or caregiver to give injections in the stomach. Dwight asked the patient if she was comfortable with the injections and she answered, "I don't know what you're talking about."

Of course Dwight became concerned, as this medication was very important for the patient's health. He asked, "Okay, is there someone at home to help you?"

The patient said, "Yes, my daughter was here but she's gone right now."

The nurse leader asked if he could get in touch with the patient's daughter by cell phone. The patient provided a phone number, and the daughter verified that they did have the medication and were helping her mother with the injections—and following all the discharge instructions.

The daughter was overwhelmed that the nurse leader, who had also visited her during the inpatient stay, had taken time to track her down and check on her mother's medications.

- Keisha, RN

This story demonstrates the power of discharge phone calls. Basically, the patient was confused about this potent medication, the nurse demonstrated care and compassion, and the family member was reassured that the hospital staff was doing a good job caring for her loved one.

The Survey Questions

This aspect of the HCAHPS survey asks three questions regarding how the hospital staff helped the patient prepare to leave the hospital. Answers are given in *yes* or *no* scale. The percent of patients who responded "yes" is publicly reported at www.hospitalcompare.hhs.gov.

Screening Question: After you left the hospital, did you go directly to your own home, to someone else's home, or to another healthcare facility?

1. During this hospital stay, did doctors, nurses, or other hospital staff talk with you about whether you would have the help you needed when you left the hospital?

2. During this hospital stay, did you get information in writing about what symptoms or health problems to look out for after you left the hospital?

The next chapters will focus on two specific tactics for the first question and one specific tactic for the second question. Evidence shows that these strategies positively impact the likelihood that patients will answer "yes" to these two questions.

This is not a laundry list of all possible tactics. Rather, it conveys a few carefully targeted specific actions you can take to immediately impact patient perception of how well your staff communicates regarding discharge instructions.

CHAPTER THIRTEEN:

STAFF DISCUSSION OF POST-DISCHARGE HELP

THE HCAHPS QUESTION: During this hospital stay, did doctors, nurses, or other hospital staff talk with you about whether you would have the help you needed when you left the hospital?

...AND THE TACTICS THAT MAKE "YES" RESPONSES MORE LIKELY

Nobody wants to go to the hospital, but if you are sick, it is the best place to be. There is a whole team of trained professionals to care for you including doctors, nurses, housekeepers, food and nutrition service staff, lab staff, respiratory therapists, and so on. But what happens when you are discharged from the hospital? These care providers certainly can't go with you!

The caregiving team must continually be asking about the help patients need when they leave the hospital. It is part of our jobs to ensure patients will have the help they need when they go home and all our staff is no longer available 24/7.

Often, a doctor can provide an estimate of how long a typical patient will stay in the hospital. This "potential" discharge date can be discussed early in the admission assessment. This demonstrates respect for the family and caregivers. Plus, knowing this date in advance helps to prevent family members from having to scramble at the last minute to get time off work or get other arrangements in place, a situation that can cause the patient discharge to be delayed from morning to evening. (And evening discharges are less than ideal for a variety of reasons.)

Plenty of research shows that if complications are going to happen, they happen within the first 72 hours after a patient is discharged from the hospital. When she and her family have a discharge date in mind, they can plan for it and have preparations in place—which minimizes the likelihood of complications and ensures that someone is there to deal with them should they occur.

One study found 44 percent of patients were not aware of their anticipated discharge dates. (O'Leary, Kevin J., et al. "Hospitalized Patients' Understanding of Their Plan of Care." *Mayo Clinic Proceedings* 85, no. 1 (2010): 47-52.) To avoid this scenario, we focus this chapter on integrating key words into the discharge process to ensure that the patient not only has an anticipated discharge date, but that she has the help she needs at home and is knowledgeable about needed information.

Once the patient has been discharged, a post-visit call can ensure she has a safe transition home and is following the discharge instructions appropriately. It also allows you to reassess and re-inform the patient about side effects to watch out for, to check on her pain level, and to make sure she has made any needed follow-up appointments.

Tactic 1: Use Key Words to Convey Discharge Information

Key words are all about "connecting the dots" with the patient. What we say and the way we say it have a tremendous impact on whether the patient will remember and understand the importance of the information.

As the patient goes through her hospital stay, key words are used to keep her thinking about her discharge date and to connect information she receives throughout her stay to what she'll need when it's time to go home. Key words can also be used to "trigger" the patient that this information is important for her discharge.

Key words also can and should be used with the patient's family and caregivers as often as possible. Family-centered care is important in all areas, but especially with discharge instructions since family will play a key role in the patient's healing process at home.

Targeted questions help the patient clarify the help she will need and who will be helping her. They also convey empathy and compassion.

"I want to make sure you and your family are prepared for your care after discharge. Can you tell me what your plans are for Tuesday when we are anticipating you will get to leave us?"

"Let me tell you about an important call. I'm going to call you at home tomorrow because I want to check on you and make sure you are okay. Can you tell me what number will be the best to reach you at?"

Here are some tips and key words that help you reinforce the importance of going home:

- **Set the stage for discharge during the admission process.** Use statements like, "We begin planning for your discharge when you're admitted..." This lets the patient know throughout her stay you'll be sharing information she needs upon discharge. Many of our high-performing hospitals have expanded the admission assessment to help prepare for potential discharge. They include tactics like performing a complete medication reconciliation, identifying who the primary caregiver will be upon discharge, and ensuring that this person is present for educational sessions. They also identify potential "core measure patients" who require specific education and discharge instructions.

- **Conduct multi-disciplinary rounds.** This team approach allows you to provide a continuum of care to the patient. Include families in case management conversations to allow the patient to be discharged in the safest and most efficient manner.

- **Remember:** *Plan for Day; Plan for Stay.* Our best performing partners have nurses discuss the plan for the day and the plan for the patient stay. In fact, these easy-to-remember phrases are written on the patient's whiteboard. (The use of a whiteboard for communicating important information about the patient's care plan is a best practice. You can write on it the anticipated day of discharge as well as the name of the person who will be helping the patient at home—with the patient's permission of course.) A discussion takes place daily about the goals for that day as well as what needs to be accomplished for the patient to be discharged.

- **Use open-ended questions.** Ask the patient open-ended questions regarding her help at home to gather more in-depth information.
    - "Can you tell me about the person who will be helping you at home?"
    - "What is your biggest concern about going home? Knowing you are going home with a walker, do have any concerns about this? How will you be accessing the bathroom? (bedroom? kitchen?)"
    - "What do you know about the special diet your doctor wants you to follow when you go home?"
    - "You will be going home on this medication, so can you tell me who will be helping you with it at home?"

- **Use key words.** Incorporate key words about discharge into the Bedside Shift Report^{SM}. The report is done in front of the patient (and involves her).

Key words can be used to ensure alignment with care providers and the patient and her family.

- o "Mrs. Jones and I reviewed some of her discharge instructions because she is going home tomorrow. We need to ask the doctor about physical therapy orders, though. Will you please check on that when he rounds later today?"

- o "Doctor Hill said during his rounds today that if the chest x-ray looks clear tomorrow, she can go home. We will want to make sure and go over her medications again tonight while her daughter is visiting."

- **Engage the family members and key caregivers in discharge instructions.**
  - o "We want you to feel comfortable taking care of your mom when she is discharged. We know you will do a great job and we will answer any questions you have about her care."
  - o "It can be pretty unsettling when we've been taking care of your mom for two weeks and now she's going home and it's going to be up to you. I want you to know that we're here to teach you how to transfer your mom from the wheelchair to the bed, and we'll be working with you to make sure you're comfortable doing that."

- **Manage patient expectations regarding length-of-stay issues.**
  - ○ Share estimated length of stay with the patient to give her an idea of when to have support lined up.
    - - "During rounds, Dr. Smith said you would be here about three days. Let's start planning for you to go home now so we are ready as soon as you are healthy enough to go home. Can you tell me who will be helping you at home?"
  - ○ Engage case management early on if there is a potential barrier to a patient being discharged home at the earliest date possible. Share these concerns with the attending physician as well.

- **Ask for agreement on discharge instructions.** Sometimes a patient will have an unarticulated fear, reservation, or uncertainty about a recommendation. If it's left unaddressed, the patient may leave the hospital and just not comply with the discharge instructions. Ask for her agreement with the instructions.
  - ○ "Do you understand and agree with these instructions? I want to make sure that you are comfortable with these recommendations."

  This should be asked again at the actual time of discharge.

- **Paraphrase key discharge instructions.** Ask the primary caregiver and the patient to repeat back information they learned through discharge instruction conversations. This powerful teaching modality can help identify potential gaps in understanding, fears, concerns, or opportunities to re-educate.
    - "Can you share the first three things you will do when you are discharged home? Can you tell me why the home care nurse will be coming on Monday? Can you tell me what you learned about the importance of smoking cessation?"

    Document these responses in the patient education record.

Tactic 2: Implement Post-Visit Phone Calls

Nurses feel better knowing their patients are prepared for discharge and have in place all the help they need to create the best healing environment. Unfortunately, research tells us that is often not the case. One study found that 81 percent of patients requiring assistance with basic functional needs failed to receive a home care referral, and 65 percent said no one at the hospital talked to them about managing their care at home. (Clark, Paul Alexander, et al. "Patient Perceptions of Quality in Discharge Instruction." *Patient Education and Counseling* 59, no. 1 (2005): 56-68.) Post-visit phone calls help us identify and resolve such situations.

These calls have evolved from a satisfaction initiative where nurses felt good calling the patients to ensure they were home safe and sound to a far more quality-based tactic. Evidence has proven that those patients who receive a post-discharge call are more satisfied with their overall experience with the hospital, but we have learned that they also can help ensure clinical quality outcomes.

Now, with hospitals potentially being financially penalized for failure to perform on certain key metrics, hospitals that have truly hardwired effective post-visit calls will see an additional benefit—reduced readmissions.

Post-visit phone calls offer the opportunity to check in on patients and make sure that they are okay and have the help they need. Studer Group has detailed resources devoted to helping healthcare organizations implement post-visit (discharge) phone calls, including Patient Call Manager, a clinical call software system that automates and documents the process to have real-time impact.

Here are a few tips that we believe will impact the patient perception of staff asking about the help they'd need after discharge.

Before you call:

- **Set expectations for the call.** Share with patients that they will receive a phone call within 24-48 hours of discharge. Many hospitals are asking the patient to confirm a convenient block of time for the call as well as the phone number where he can be reached. Many times, patients will not go to their own homes, or, in some short-stay cases, they will already be back at work within the calling time frame.

- ○ Note: Many of our partner hospitals have found that patients provide cell numbers and this makes it easier to check on the patient regardless of where he is. These "new" phone numbers patients are providing nursing have also been helpful to the business office in aiding collections and lowering bad debt.

- **Collect questions.** As you are preparing the patient for discharge, remind him that you'll be calling to check in on him. Ask him to write down questions he may have once he's home so that you can answer them when you call.

When you call:

- **Verify discharge instructions.** Always make sure the patient understands his discharge instructions. "When you were discharged, Becky went over your discharge instructions with you. She asked you about the three priorities you were going to take care of when you got home. Can you share with me what you have done since you've been home with regard to your three priorities?"
  - ○ **Ask probing questions and dig deeper to gain insight.** "Have you filled your prescription yet? Where you able to change your bandage? Has home care contacted you?"

- ○ **Access patient records.** If possible, pull up the patient's records to refer to during the call. It's very helpful to have those discharge instructions in front of you.

- **Focus on care and follow-up.** Ensure the discharge questions are about quality care and follow-up at home and are not intended to bias the patient or compete with any of the HCAHPS survey questions. Ask open-ended questions. Some examples to use include:
  - ○ "Are you as comfortable as you can be right now? How is your pain now, compared to when you were in the hospital?"
  - ○ "Do you have any questions about your medications?"
  - ○ "Have you made/kept (or when is) your follow-up appointment with your doctor or clinic?"
  - ○ "May I ask how your nursing care was?"
  - ○ "We like to recognize our employees, volunteers, and physicians who provide exceptional care. Is there anyone you would like to recognize?"

- **Focus on clinical.** The post-visit call is the perfect time to speak about clinical indicators including:
  - ○ Ask if the patient understands his self-care instructions, medication uses, doses, and side effects.

- If appropriate, probe for indicators of infection, such as swelling, redness, fever, and so forth.
- Confirm compliance and understanding of discharge instructions.
- Remind the patient to schedule a follow-up appointment with his physician and to call with any questions.

- **Validate!** If appropriate, pick one focus area in which to validate staff actions on discharge phone calls. This will help evaluate the patient perception of hardwired processes such as hand washing, ID checks, and so forth.
  - "Did you see staff washing their hands before they touched you?" Or, "How often...?"
  - "Did the staff check your ID band before giving you medication?" Or, "How often...?"

- **Set some goals.** You may wish to set some goals for discharge calls. A sample goal might be 100 percent attempted, 80 percent reached. We suggest you make up to three attempts within the first 48 hours. (Note: We have found calls after 72 hours are considered more of a nuisance than a help by patients.)

Key Words at Key Times and post-visit phone calls allow you to tell the patient what he needs to know about his transition home—and then follow up with him to ensure he's doing what he needs to be doing. Together, these tactics help you make his transition as smooth, as comfortable, and most important of all *as safe* as possible.

Tools & Resources

Studer Group offers a variety of tools and resources that support the tactics discussed in this chapter. To access the most up-to-date offerings, please visit www.studergroup.com/HCAHPS.

CHAPTER FOURTEEN:

WRITTEN SYMPTOM/ HEALTH PROBLEM INFORMATION

THE HCAHPS QUESTION: During this hospital stay, did you get information in writing about what symptoms or health problems to look out for after you left the hospital?

...AND THE TACTICS THAT MAKE "YES" RESPONSES MORE LIKELY

When patients leave the hospital, it is important they have the material and information needed for their care at home. Staff may have done an excellent job of preparing the patient but she will still need materials to reference just in case. It is similar to keeping a favorite recipe filed away: You're pretty sure you could make it without the written recipe, but it is certainly reassuring to have it to reference. Providing written information at discharge is a way to reassure the patient by giving her a reference to check back to.

Most organizations enclose this written symptom and health information in a discharge folder that contains all kinds of relevant information and brochures about the hospital or services. Typically, this is placed at the patient's bedside...and rarely looked at again except for when she wants to know what the TV channels are or how to place a long distance phone call.

Our job is to provide patients this information in a way that ensures they can easily find the most important points. The discharge folder is a good storage spot for all the patient information...but how can we make it more effective? The answer is below.

Tactic 1: Provide Patient-Friendly Educational Materials

All too often, we hear about patients going home with a full packet of instructions—yet, when a care provider calls to ask, they say, "I never got any instructions." If you've ever had a baby, you can probably relate. You were almost certainly discharged from the hospital with a folder filled with information. Now ask yourself, *Where is the folder? Did the folder ever get opened? And if it did, was there just too much information?* See our point?

Below are tactics to make the patient education materials more effective.

- **Use bright colors and clearly marked labels.** Create brightly colored discharge instruction folders, clearly labeled "Discharge Instructions." We find that high-performing organizations also add

CHAPTER FOURTEEN: WRITTEN SYMPTOM INFORMATION

"Including Current Medications" to the label. The folders or envelopes should be given at admission or during the admission assessment so patients know they are an important piece of healthcare information. They should be referenced by all caregivers who hand out any relevant patient information.

- **Treat the folder like it's important and the patient will as well.** Let the patient know that this folder will hold important documents that she may need to reference while she's in the hospital—but will certainly need to reference upon discharge. Keep in it all important information on activity level, diet, medication side effects, follow up appointments, and symptoms to look out for after discharge. Other information such as smoking cessation information can be included as well to increase compliance with core measures.

Don't just leave the folder on the bedside table. It will get lost in the shuffle. Draw the patient's attention to it as you add information to it throughout the patient's stay. If the team ensures the folder is kept as an important part of the care plan, the patient will pay attention to it as well.

- **Design the folder for action.** This folder is about the patient and not the hospital. It is not a marketing brochure. It should be clearly labeled "Discharge Instructions." Some of our partners add a label to the front with a space to write "Top three things to do when I get home…" If you do this, be sure to include a space to write these items down. As you and the patient talk about discharge, ask the patient (if possible) or the patient's at-home caregiver to write down the three most important to-dos.

- **Build off an ED discharge instruction format.** Use a best practice from the Emergency Department on discharge instructions. Create a sheet of paper with the top boldly labeled "DISCHARGE INSTRUCTIONS/MEDICATION SIDE EFFECTS." Include a spot for each of the following: "Reasons to call doctor, Side effects to watch for, Patient priorities, and Follow-up needed." Some organizations also summarize the key patient roles and to-dos. The patient signs that she understands and will follow through.

You might ask the patient to repeat back the important items she just learned. The point is to engage the patient and/or family member as an active participant in her care.

- **Align these materials with core measures.** Identify potential core measure patients at admission. This will ensure all care plans and processes include diagnosis-specific information that's shared and tracked appropriately. An example of this would be heart failure patients who need written instructions around medications, diet, activity, follow-up appointment, weight gain, and what to do if heart failure symptoms worsen.

- **Share daily medication schedules with the patient.** Some hospitals create a daily hospital medication schedule for each patient. A copy of this schedule can be kept in the patient's folder for quick reference, and, of course, a final "schedule" will be given to the patient upon discharge after appropriate medication reconciliation. Daily medication schedules usually have grids to help the patient identify dosage and timing of medications. They also include medications she was taking at home and any medications that she was previously taking but that have been discontinued. These schedules help prevent medication errors and elevate compliance.

- **Highlight key points.** When discharge information or medication sheets are provided to the patient or the at-home caregiver, have her highlight key information. This will serve as an easy reference for the future regarding points that were important to her.

- **Don't let paper replace human interaction.** Discharge instructions are becoming very detailed, but we can't let a piece of paper talk for us. Nothing takes the place of explaining instructions to the patient person-to-person. Hopefully you've covered the information in the discharge folder at various points during the patient's stay—but review the entire folder with her again at the actual time of discharge. (You can have this conversation at the same time that you discuss the post-visit phone calls.)

- **Train those who escort the patient at discharge to notice the folder.**
  - The person might say: "Here is your discharge folder—I want you to carry it out so you will have it handy. It has lots of important information so make sure and put it in a safe and convenient place when you get home."

Having a thorough, well-organized, reader-friendly written record of what patients should do once they get home makes compliance far more likely. Thus, these materials go a long way toward improving clinical outcomes and reducing avoidable rehospitalizations—both of which are even more important than improving HCAHPS results.

Tools & Resources

Studer Group offers a variety of tools and resources that support the tactics discussed in this chapter. To access the most up-to-date offerings, please visit www.studergroup.com/HCAHPS.

To follow is a worksheet that will help you create a plan to improve patient perception of care in the "discharge information" arena.

The discharge process in most hospitals is a giant opportunity for improvement. The more we can help patients achieve a safe transition home, the more we can further our mission to provide excellent care. Our patients deserve the kind of guidance and instructions that will allow them to continue this excellent care at home. Let's do all we can to provide it to them.

Discharge Information Planning Sheet

HCAHPS "TOP-BOX" PERCENTILES—December 2009 Public Reporting*

					Discharge Information Composite
Percentile among reporting hospitals	5th	25th	50th	75th	95th
Percent of *always* responses	71	77	81	84	88

* These numbers are estimates based on historic national percentiles.

Current Discharge Information Domain Result: _____

Converted to percentile: _____

90-Day Goal: _____ Percentile: _____

Action Plan:

HOSPITAL ENVIRONMENT (CLEAN & QUIET)

A s healthcare professionals, we'll go to great lengths to help patients get the best outcomes. We'll make sure they have the right medications, get the appropriate tests, and know we care. We'll respond quickly and efficiently to their requests. We'll make sure they know what to do after they're discharged. But what about the physical environment? Are we doing everything possible to ensure that it's conducive to the healing process?

A clean, quiet hospital is vitally important. Obviously, the "clean" part can have life-or-death implications for patients. (And just as obviously, hospital-acquired infections have a profound impact on an organization's financial health.) But both cleanliness and quietness have psychological effects as well—which, in turn, impact clinical outcomes.

Ask yourself these questions:

If a post-op patient is repositioned hourly to avoid bed sores but has dirty linens on her bathroom floor, does she have increased anxiety and worry about germs?

If a patient knows his medication's name, purpose, dosage, and side effects but can't get any sleep at night due to noise and/or bright lights, will he be more anxious and irritable due to lack of sleep?

The answer to both questions is a resounding "yes."

Study after study has shown that the healthcare environment affects the well-being of patients. When asked about their rooms, patients mention the importance of such aspects of the environment as cleanliness, comfort, and privacy. (Bruster, S., et al. "National Survey of Hospital Patients." *British Medical Journal* 309 (1994): 1542.) When this healing environment doesn't exist, psychological stress can build in the patient and can negatively affect healing and wellness. (Ulrich, R. S. "Effects of Interior Design on Wellness: Theory and Recent Scientific Research." *Journal of Health Care Interior Design* 3 (1991): 97-109.)

So, what can we do to provide a healing environment for our patients? For starters, we can focus on the patients' perception of how often we have "always" kept their rooms and bathrooms clean and kept their rooms quiet at night. The Hospital Environment composite of the HCAHPS survey allows us to measure just how well we are doing in the eyes of patients.

The chapters that follow will share tactics that have helped the organizations Studer Group® works with achieve outcomes well above those of the nation.

But first, here's a story that shares the impact a quiet and clean environment can have on the patient.

On our unit we were very focused on our environmental service workers asking for input from our patients. One of our unit housekeepers, Betty, took to this practice naturally and has made a tremendous difference. Here is just one patient example:

Housekeeper Betty entered Mrs. Mendelssohn's room. Betty acknowledged Mrs. Mendelssohn, introduced herself, and began to perform her duties.

Although Betty was unaware of Mrs. Mendelssohn's history, she had been readmitted to the hospital for additional treatment related to a post-op infection she had developed on her prior admission. Given her history of a hospital-acquired infection, the patient was both concerned about and acutely aware of cleanliness.

When Betty finished her duties, she stated, "Mrs. Mendelssohn, I need you to help me keep your room clean by telling me if I've missed anything."

Mrs. Mendelssohn replied, "No, not that I see."

Betty then asked, "Can I move something to a new spot to make it easier on you?"

She replied, "No, I can't think of anything."

Betty again asked, "Before I leave, can you again look and see if I missed anything?"

"You even got that cotton ball under my roommate's bed," Mrs. Mendelssohn replied. "I have been watching it for three days.

"You are the first person who has asked me that question," she added. *"They must have told you I am very concerned about getting another infection."*

Betty replied, *"No, ma'am. I'm just helping provide excellent care."*

While the room was cleaned, it was Betty's approach that made a change in the patient's perception.

- *Frieda S., RN*

This story sheds light on how deeply aware patients are of the hospital environment. As Mrs. Mendelssohn's "cotton ball vigil" attests, they notice when we're doing a good job of keeping things clean—and when we're not. They're also acutely sensitive to how quiet and restful the hospital is. When we hardwire tactics to keep our hospital clean and quiet, we can positively impact patients' perception of their healing environment.

The Survey Questions

These two questions are on the HCAHPS survey for the patient perception of the "hospital environment" arena. Answers are given in frequency scale: *never, sometimes, usually,* or *always.* The percent of patients who responded "always" is publicly reported at www.hospitalcompare. hhs.gov.

1. During this hospital stay, how often were your room and bathroom kept clean?

2. During this hospital stay, how often was the area around your room quiet at night?

In the chapters that follow, we will share the specific tactics for each question that positively impact the likelihood that patients will answer "always" to these two questions.

This is not a laundry list of all possible tactics. Rather, it conveys a few carefully targeted specific actions you can take to immediately impact patient perception of the cleanliness and quietness of your hospital.

NOTE: While we understand these two questions are reported separately, we believe they both contribute to a healing environment. That's why, though we recognize they're not presented together in reports, we've opted to address them together in this book. Additionally, this handbook is not intended to address processes for reducing infections and protocols for actually cleaning a room.

Chapter Fifteen:

Nighttime Quietness

THE HCAHPS QUESTION: During this hospital stay, how often was the area around your room quiet at night?

Hospitals are busy places. They certainly aren't the kind of business that can close the doors and shut off the lights at 9 p.m. Patients need assistance 24 hours a day, 7 days a week. There are late admissions and discharges, medication to be given, dressings to be changed, and so forth. There are family members and friends of patients coming and going at all hours. And, of course, the floors need to be cleaned, lightbulbs changed, and equipment transferred.

What's more, patients can hear all the noises that hospital staff members have grown accustomed to. They may even be bothered by noises we can't hear at all! Consider also that regardless of how the question is worded, if the hospital is noisy and chaotic during the day, patients will not perceive it to be a healing environment.

In view of all these realities, is it possible for hospitals to create a quiet environment at night for patients? The answer is yes, we can—or at least we can create a *quieter* environment. For many patients sleep is an important part of their recovery…and we owe it to them to ensure that they get as much as they possibly can.

…AND THE TACTICS THAT MAKE "ALWAYS" RESPONSES MORE LIKELY

In almost all cases, a reduction of activity is required to achieve a quiet environment. In a hospital environment, that is very hard to do. But there are many things that can be done to reduce the noise in the areas around patient rooms.

We have found our highest performers have instilled a level of sensitivity and accountability around noise management into their own staff. Staff members in these organizations are completely willing to confront loud behaviors whether it is coming from each other or physicians.

That said, we have found that there is not one overarching tactic that impacts this question. Instead, it is a combination of the little things.

Tips for impacting the "quiet at night" question:

- **Perform a noise audit.** Assign leaders to conduct "secret shopping" with the intent of "listening" for improvement opportunities as they relate to noise at night. Have them pay special attention to staff voices and noisy equipment that needs immediate attention. Things that may seem like "normal business" to staff—squeaky wheels on carts, chart assembly with binders opening and closing, linen closet door hinges clanging, ringing telephones—can be incredibly irritating to patients. (Have you ever stayed in a hotel where just the sound of doors opening and closing is irritating? If so, you can imagine how patients feel.)

- ○ Ask a leader to be a "patient for a night." You'll be surprised at the noise the volunteer reports back. We've found that patients hear a lot of conversations between nurses and other hospital staff.

- **Close the doors as often as possible.** Of course, safety comes first, but when possible, at least partially close doors to protect privacy and hold out noise as well. This has been shown to be the number one tactic to reducing noise and enhancing patient perception of hospital quietness. Formal "close the doors" campaigns have proven to raise HCAHPS results dramatically in the first quarter. So, if you pick one thing to implement for this question, implement "close the doors."

  - ○ Make standard at exit: Train all staff to close the door upon exiting a room.

- Use key words when closing the door: "I am going to close the door for your privacy and so you can rest better."
- Use key words when leaving the door open: For patients who express the desire to keep their doors open, use key words. "I am happy to leave the door open, but it may be noisy; are you sure?"
- Address exceptions: For clinical situations where the door may need to stay open—fall risk, clinically unstable, etc.—develop a system to notify staff of this. One organization places a star on the door frame of patients whose doors need to remain open.

- **"Bunch" nighttime tasks together.** This helps ensure that patients are not woken up during the night more often than absolutely necessary. Also, explain nighttime Hourly Rounding^SM to patients and make sure staff are sensitive to quiet rounds.

- **Adapt key rounding questions for leaders.** The idea is to demonstrate compassion and empathy around resting.
  - "I know it can be hard to get sleep in the hospital. Can you tell me if you got some good rest last night?" Or, "We want you to heal quickly. How well did you rest last night?"

- **Use bed management teams to protect privacy.** When census allows, keep rooms private until absolutely necessary. Also identify the "loudest" rooms, like those by elevators, main thoroughfares, or staff lounges, and fill them last.

- **Adapt patient-centered visiting guidelines.** While we are strong proponents of family-centered care and open visitation regarding hours, this does not mean that patients can have ten visitors at the bedside at all times. Patient-centered visitation should not come at the expense of other patients' ability to rest. Train all staff on dealing with the (usually minor) problems relating to excess visitation.

- **Manage nighttime lab draws.** This can be done with key words or a varied schedule.
  - Often patients are woken up in the middle of the night for a lab draw. If this needs to happen, share the *why* with the patient: "I'm going to need to wake you in the night for a lab draw. I hate to wake you, but it is important that the test be done and on your chart by the time the doctor rounds in the morning."

- **Dim the lights.** Just lowering the lighting can naturally get staff to talk more softly. Even better news: You'll save on electricity. (This will contribute to your efforts to be more green.)

- **Use "SHH" signs.** These do a great job of reminding patients, family, and staff about the focus on creating a healing environment. Engage physicians and staff and change the posters regularly so they are new and noticeable. For physicians, have the signs read, "Doctors' Orders: Our Patients Are Resting" or something else fun and creative. Place them by loud areas like elevators and nursing stations.

- **Meet with EVS to address squeaky wheels and other maintenance noise.** Changing to soft wheels on noisy dollies and linen carts is usually one of the first items on an action plan and definitely worth the investment.

- **Eliminate overhead paging and paging into patient rooms from the desk unless absolutely necessary.** Discuss the "volume" of overhead paging if this is an issue.

- **Provide "noise reduction" tools such as headphones and earplugs.** Earplugs are inexpensive and a good "band-aid" but do not address the root cause. Headphones can often be plugged into the pillow speakers for background noise. Soothing music is a research-based complementary strategy for reducing pain and stress or anxiety. If you encourage patients to bring their own music for distraction, be careful about tracking any ipods, MP3 players, etc. as valuables.

- **If you use items like "Yacker Trackers," make sure they're not a substitute for human monitoring of noisy staff behaviors.** Ensure staff members are trained that these electronic devices (available through multiple vendors) are just visual representations of our efforts to raise awareness of noise levels. Engage night supervisors to monitor the Yacker Tracker for appropriate placement, volume monitor, and compliance when it goes off—these "awareness raisers" are only as good as the people who pay attention and change their behaviors based on the information. The best unit to see value from the Yacker Tracker is the NICU where a quiet environment is essential.

- **Develop key words for noisy occasions.** These will help staff members deal with problems related to noisy roommates, family issues, or construction.
    - "We want to provide the best healing environment for all our patients. Would you mind lowering your noise level to help our other patients get the rest they need?"

- **Connect the dots on *why* we care about noise.** It is not enough to implement strategies like Yacker Trackers, headphones, and so forth without telling the patients about the goal to create a quiet environment.
    - "We want to keep your room quiet at night so you can rest—would you like us to close your door? We will be in to check on you

approximately every two hours during the night."

- "We do our best to keep it quiet for you, especially at night, but sometimes it is noisy as we care for our patients. Would you like some ear plugs to help you rest better?"
- "Sometimes our voices seem louder at night, so please let us know if we are bothering you or if you cannot sleep."
- "I am checking this pump now, so hopefully it won't alarm you in the night."

A quiet environment is a healing environment. By taking steps to lower your nighttime noise level, you help patients reduce stress, get plenty of restful sleep, and ultimately enjoy better clinical outcomes.

Tools & Resources

Studer Group offers a variety of tools and resources that support the tactics discussed in this chapter. To access the most up-to-date offerings, please visit www.studergroup.com/HCAHPS.

CHAPTER SIXTEEN:

ROOM AND BATHROOM CLEANLINESS

THE HCAHPS QUESTION: During this hospital stay, how often were your room and bathroom kept clean?

Most of us would do just about anything to avoid using most gas station restrooms. Some of us would do almost anything to avoid using any public restroom. Why? Plain and simple...we think they are dirty. Sometimes, it is dirt we can see. Other times, we can visualize the microscopic germs on every single surface. What we're really afraid of is getting some infection or disease.

Now, imagine how patients feel about such germs—real or imagined—in a hospital setting.

Cleanliness matters. It especially matters at a hospital when germs can cause infections that can have a profound impact on our patients. This HCAHPS question may focus just on patients' rooms and bathrooms, but their perception of their experience is definitely impacted by other areas, so a focus on overall organizational cleanliness is critical.

And cleanliness isn't just about housekeeping or environmental services. All staff own this HCAHPS question and can impact it by reducing clutter, picking up trash, and so forth. They can demonstrate courtesy and respect at the same time by treating the patient room like it is their guest bedroom and the patient like she is their guest.

...AND THE TACTICS THAT MAKE "ALWAYS" RESPONSES MORE LIKELY

How can we demonstrate to our patients the importance we place on keeping their rooms and bathrooms clean? Below are two tactics that will make a difference in the patients' perception of cleanliness.

Before we jump into these tactics, please be aware that clean doesn't mean new. Some of our partners with the oldest hospitals perform best on this HCAHPS question.

Tactic 1: Conduct Environmental Leader Rounding

There is no better way of finding out if you are truly serving your customers than by asking them directly. Environmental leader rounding allows you to check in with nursing leaders and directly with patients to gain insight into what is working well and what can be improved. It is a chance for a leader from environmental services to verify that the room and bathroom are clean and to rec- ognize staff members who do a good job and coach those who need improvement. It also lets patients know provid- ing them with a clean, healing environment is a priority.

We've found that, for any patient who has an issue regarding cleanliness, rounding again by the leaders of EVS increases the opportunity to change her perception to excellent by addressing any issues in real time. Just checking back in to be sure the issue was resolved helps patients and their families feel they are cared about.

Here are some rounding tips for environmental services leaders:

- **Practice looking through their eyes.** As you round (or just walk through the facility), look through the eyes of the patients and their families. Remember that patients are lying in a bed, so don't forget to look at the ceiling. You might not immedi- ately notice the stained grout in the bathroom, but a patient or family member definitely will.

- **Round first on the unit manager and establish a rounding plan.** This should include frequency of patient rounding and a follow-up pro- cess to be used if a problem is identified.

- **Make it manageable.** One hundred percent rounding on all patients daily can be difficult de- pending on resources and size of facility. Pick a number and round randomly for spot checks. Start with the lower-performing units and those with the largest number of admissions and discharges first.

- **Always round on the manager first.** This will help ensure it is an appropriate time, it will help you learn about any service recovery opportunities, and it will allow you to make sure you are not "over-rounding and bothering" patients with the same questions.

- **As you round...**
  - **Ask questions.** Question the patient about the cleanliness of her room. (See key words below.)
  - **Check for cleanliness.** Check the bathroom before you leave using the key words, "May I check your bathroom?" After checking, say, "(Name of housekeeper) did a very good job of cleaning and sanitizing it for your safety." (Note: If the bathroom is not clean, address it right away.)
  - **Leave contact information.** Leave your card and indicate that you are available if at any time the patient feels the room and bathroom are not consistently clean. Tell her you will check in again tomorrow to follow up.
  - **Build in recognition.** Ask if there's any staff member who should be recognized. Immediately follow up with the staff to reward or coach to higher performance.

- ○ **Follow up on any concerns.** If a patient concern is identified, follow up with the patient—and the nursing staff.

- **Use key words that speak to cleanliness.** When rounding on the patient, build in words like "clean" and "sanitized." Below is a sample of key words for an EVS leader rounding on a patient:
  - ○ Knock on door. "Hi, my name is Benjamin. I am the director of environmental services here at I-Care Hospital. (Greet the family.) May I have a few minutes of your time to ask you a few questions? Is this a good time?" (If not, say, "I am sorry to have disturbed you. I will try again at a better time.") "At I-Care Hospital, it is important to us that we do a very good job of cleaning your room and bathroom."
  - ○ "Vanessa is your housekeeper. She is one of our best and always does a very good job of not only cleaning but also sanitizing the room for your safety. Did Vanessa introduce herself when she came into your room?" (If you find she does this consistently, then change the question when you round the next time to validate duration (i.e., "Did she tell you how long it would take for her to clean your room?").

    If housekeeper gets a compliment, tell the patient, "I will be sure to let Vanessa know—I am sure she will be very pleased!"

- Ask family members: "How have you found the cleanliness of the hospital?"
- "Would you mind if I checked your bathroom to make sure everything is in order and we did a very good job of cleaning it?" If everything is okay, say, "Vanessa did a very good job." If not, say, "I would like Vanessa to stop back by to be sure it is very clean."
- "Is there anything we missed? Is there anything else we can do to improve your stay?"
- "Let me leave you my business card. This is the number you may call if you have any issues with our Environmental Services Department. Call if at any time we are not consistently doing a very good job with cleaning your room and bathroom." Or, if a number is already available, review it with the patient: "I see Vanessa's name and number are on the whiteboard as well."
- "Thank you for your time. I will check back in with you tomorrow!"

- **Regularly round on the key nursing units. Document outcomes.** The following examples reflect approaches used by EVS directors to get feedback, share desired actions, and communicate outcomes on HCAHPS results with leaders:
  - "What is working well with EVS?" (Sometimes a simple question can help you glean valuable insights into potential prob-

lems or can help identify best practices to harvest and move to other areas.)

- o "I noticed your 'patient perception of cleanliness' rating is above our hospital's goal. We perform far better than most other hospitals across the nation in terms of patients feeling that their rooms were always kept clean, and I want you to know that your team is a big part of that."

- o "Our paper toilet seat covers will be installed in all semi-private rooms on September first. In your opinion, is there anything specific I can do to help improve the patient perception of cleanliness on your unit?"

- o "Do you have any suggestions on how we can improve our cleanliness on your unit or in your department?"

- **Use specific reward and recognition from the survey results as available.**
  - o "The HCAHPS result has improved to 90 percent of patients saying the room was always kept clean. I think Jane has a big role in these overall results, so would you please make sure she knows we appreciate her?"

Here are a few ideas (outside of rounding) for the EVS leader to consider:

- **Create a clean team.** This group might consist of EVS, nursing, and ancillary leaders. They would look for opportunities organization-wide to focus on cleanliness. For instance:

- ○ Ask for help: Ask administration to empty their own trash so housekeepers get more time on the units.
- ○ Audit trash can locations: Review and make sure trash cans are located in the best areas.
- ○ Make sure everyone's on trash duty: Train all staff to pick up trash on the floor in the hallways.

- **Connect the dots with the housekeeping staff.** Be sure they understand they aren't simply cleaning rooms. Many times they are the first line of defense in stopping infections. Teach EVS workers about MRSA and other organisms and their role in stopping them from spreading. This will improve the consistency of cleaning something even when it looks clean.

- **Don't forget the importance of cleaning "other items" like the telephone, remote control, and call button.** These can harbor germs just like any other surface.

- **Assign housekeepers to units.** Organizations do better on this composite if the housekeepers are part of the nursing unit team.

- **Deploy resources to enable patients to experience multiple housekeeping**

encounters. One hospital that we work with altered the housekeepers' assignment, so that patients had four encounters with housekeeping each day. Here's how it works:

- o When housekeeper arrives on unit at start of shift, she empties patient room trash. This is used as an opportunity for the housekeeper to introduce herself and let the patient know she will return later in the day to clean and sanitize the room and bathroom.
- o Housekeeper returns for full room cleaning. She uses prescribed key words and behaviors.
- o The housekeeping leader rounds on patient using key words described earlier.
- o At end of shift, housekeeper checks with patient on room cleanliness, empties trash, and refreshes towels if needed.

- **Build EVS evaluation goals around the HCAHPS "cleanliness" question and infection control.** For example, a goal might be to "Increase percent *always* to 85th percentile for 'Room and Bathroom Kept Clean' composite as measured by HCAHPS." At some organizations, housekeepers are assigned to units and have goals related to each particular unit's results.

Tactic 2: Use Key Words at Key Times

We want our patients to get a consistent message: "We care about you and want to provide a healing environment for you." Key words are the best tool for standardizing communication to consistently demonstrate care and concern for the patient.

Key words can also reduce anxiety for those staff members who are not accustomed to speaking with patients. Our top-performing hospitals have invested the time and resources to train all environmental staff to have actual conversations with patients. In many cases we're taking people completely out of their comfort zones. For them, key words are a lifeline.

Key words also help to connect people with the *why*—why you want them talking to a patient in the first place. Ask them, "If that were your mom in there and someone was cleaning her room, would you want that person to talk to her? If your mom was sitting by the bedside and a housekeeper came in to clean, would you want that housekeeper to speak to her?"

Of course the answer is yes, and when housekeeping staff members hear it explained in this way, they almost always get on board.

We've got to let staff know that it's good to talk to patients—and they need a minimum level of communication skills to be in a patient room.

A few tips:

- **Train staff to ask permission to clean.**
  - They should knock prior to entering and say, "Hello, Mr. Jones. I am Oscar and I will be cleaning your room and bathroom. It will

take about ten minutes. Is now a good time for me to come in? Thank you. Before I begin I just want to wash my hands."

This is another way to ensure the patient and family know that cleanliness and handwashing is expected of all staff, not just nursing.

- **Teach key words around cleanliness.** For example:
  - ○ "We want to make sure your room and bathroom are always clean and sanitized—is there anything I've missed?"
  - ○ "I've cleaned your bathroom and noticed an area that needs to be repaired in the shower."
  - ○ "Let me go ahead and empty your trash can because I see it is getting full and we want your room to be clean."

- **Give EVS team permission to talk to and connect with patients.** Set the expectation that they will treat patients with a minimum level of courtesy and respect. They can and should proactively ask how patients are feeling, address the family members, and offer to do small acts of kindness for patients or their families if appropriate.

- **Empower the EVS team to resolve problems.** For example, if when cleaning a room the housekeeper notices a leaking faucet, have him request it be repaired.

- "Mr. Rodriguez, I noticed the faucet on your sink is dripping. I hope it hasn't been disturbing you. I will contact engineering and ask that they repair it as soon as possible. I will check back to ensure it has been taken care of."

- **Give the patient some control in determining time for cleaning.** Ask, "Is now a good time for me to clean your room?"
  - If the patient is eating, say, "I see you are eating dinner. May I start in your bathroom?"

- **Engage the family.** "Your mom's room looks clean. Does anyone see anything I missed?" Make eye contact with the patient and any visitors in the room.

- **Establish a consistent routine.** Housekeepers should have a consistent list and order for cleaning their rooms. This will build good habits and ensure that steps aren't missed. They can also build in key words to reinforce the action with the patient and build a relationship. Here are some examples of steps and key words to go with them:
  - Remove soiled linens and trash. "Let me get you some fresh linens and empty your wastebaskets. Do you have anything you'd like me to take?"
  - Sanitize and wipe down surfaces. "Mr. Murphy, I want to make sure your room is

sanitized so I am wiping down all surfaces. Do you see anything I missed?"
- ○ Clean bathroom. "I have cleaned and sanitized your bathroom. Please let me know if there is anything I missed."
- ○ Dust and mop floor. "I'm almost done. Is there anything you see that needs further attention? Is there anything I can do for you before I leave?"

Leaders can observe each staff member to make sure they're doing all of these steps correctly.

- **If the patient isn't in the room, make sure he knows housekeeping has been there.**
  - ○ Leave a card: Create tent cards as noticeable proof the room has been cleaned. Use key words that align with the hospital concern for cleanliness and not to introduce bias on any survey. Do *not* let tent cards become "clutter" or a replacement for actually connecting personally with the patient.
  - ○ Check back: Have the housekeeper stop back in the room and say, "I cleaned your room while you were gone. I wanted to check back and see if there was anything I missed."

- **Develop a picture tool addressing cleanliness.** This will help to improve communications with patients who may have a language barrier and thus have a difficult time understanding the goal of keeping the room clean.

- **Mention cleanliness during Hourly Rounding.** Make sure staff members *tell* patients they are checking the environment for their safety. Also, they will want to make sure the trashcan is empty and within the patient's reach and the room is orderly and uncluttered. And it's important not to leave finished dietary trays for extended periods.

- **Say it in a video.** Some high-performing organizations have created a short video for patients to watch that explains the room cleaning process and how it contributes to a safe, healing environment. You can put it on your closed-caption TV channel if you have one and ask patients and families to watch it on admission.

Patients are all too aware of the health risks associated with germs in the healthcare environment. After all, they hear the news reports and many may know people who've gotten hospital-acquired infections. They will truly appreciate your efforts to keep rooms and bathrooms clean and sanitized—and your efforts to let them know you're doing so.

Tools & Resources

Studer Group offers a variety of tools and resources that support the tactics discussed in this chapter. To access the most up-to-date offerings, please visit www.studergroup.com/HCAHPS.

To follow are worksheets that will help you create a plan to improve patient perception of care in the "cleanliness" and "quietness" arenas.

As health reform laws tighten up and hospital-acquired infections become an even more critical issue, a laser-focus on cleanliness will be paramount. But the true impetus for providing a clean environment goes far deeper than finances. We do it because we want to provide the very best place for our patients to receive care.

The same applies to "quietness."

We keep our hospitals clean and quiet because it's the right thing to do. By paying attention to the details of our physical environment, we help patients heal. There can be no more important reason to strive for *always*.

Nighttime Quietness Planning Sheet

HCAHPS "TOP-BOX" PERCENTILES—December 2009 Public Reporting*

			Nighttime Quietness Composite		
Percentile among reporting hospitals	5th	25th	50th	75th	95th
Percent of *always* responses	40	48	55	63	76

* These numbers are estimates based on historic national percentiles.

Current Nighttime Quietness Domain Result: _____

Converted to percentile: _____

90-Day Goal: _____ Percentile: _____

Action Plan:

Cleanliness Planning Sheet

HCAHPS "TOP-BOX" PERCENTILES—December 2009 Public Reporting*

					Cleanliness Composite
Percentile among reporting hospitals	5th	25th	50th	75th	95th
Percent of *always* responses	56	64	69	75	84

* These numbers are estimates based on historic national percentiles.

Current Cleanliness Domain Result: _____

Converted to percentile: _____

90-Day Goal: _____ Percentile: _____

Action Plan:

Overall Rating of Hospital and Willingness to Recommend

A ll things considered, what kind of experience do your patients have? What "grade" might they give your hospital? Are they or aren't they willing to give you the ultimate compliment and recommend you to someone else? And do they feel loyalty to your hospital—an important predictor of future utilization and revenue?

To us, a patient's overall impression may seem pretty subjective. From her perspective, though, it's objective. When we fail to give a patient an overall positive experience, it's because we haven't learned what is important to her.

A patient who gives us a less-than-perfect rating or fails to recommend us may have had positive experiences in every area covered by HCAHPS except, perhaps, for one. Maybe a stressed-out staff member spoke shortly to her or one dose of her pain medicine was late or maybe the patient next door had lots of noisy visitors who interfered with her sleep. That one small incident can color her entire experience in a negative way.

Healthcare organizations must do everything possible to ensure that every patient perceives every aspect of her care to be the best. That translates to individualized care, which yields the insight needed to keep care providers from ever being in a position where they have to say, "If only we had known."

We're pleased to say that Studer Group® partners do a great job in this area. They outperform the rest of the industry on the HCAHPS Global Rating composite by 18 percentile points and on the Willingness to Recommend composite by 20 percentile points. These results not only tie to the patients' perception of quality, but also to reportable quality metrics, as these same facilities outperform the nation on all core measures.

The Survey Questions

HCAHPS goes from asking for patient responses on specific issues like pain management to asking overarching "summary" questions. By the time the patient gets to this portion of the survey she is being asked to step back and take a broad view of her experience. It's the proverbial "at the end of the day" impression: *How good was the hospital, really? Would you want to come back here—or send someone you love here?*

This section of the HCAHPS survey asks patients about their overall perception of their stay. For the first question, which asks patients to rate the hospital, answers are given on a 0 to 10 scale. Zero denotes the "worst hospital possible" and 10 denotes the "best hospital possible." The percent of patients who give answers of 9 or 10 is publicly reported on www.hospitalcompare.hhs.gov.

1. Using any number from 0 to 10, where 0 is the worst hospital possible and 10 is the best hospital possible, what number would you use to rate this hospital during your stay?

The second question asks patients whether they would recommend the hospital to friends and family. Answers are given in *definitely no* to *definitely yes* scale. The percent of patients who give the answer *definitely yes* is publicly reported on www.hospitalcompare.hhs.gov.

2. Would you recommend this hospital to your friends and family?

In the chapter that follows, we will discuss an overarching approach and a few tips that, together, positively impact the likelihood that patients will respond with a "9 or 10" and a "definitely yes," respectively.

CHAPTER SEVENTEEN:

OVERALL RATING/ WILLINGNESS TO RECOMMEND

The HCAHPS QUESTION: Using any number from 0 to 10, where 0 is the worst hospital possible and 10 is the best hospital possible, what number would you use to rate this hospital during your stay?

Every experience your patient has during his stay factors into his overall evaluative perspective of your hospital. It all counts: how well nurses (and everyone else) communicated with him...how physicians treated him...how responsive staff members were when he asked for something...how well his pain was managed...how clearly his medication was explained...how discharge instructions were handled...and how clean and quiet the hospital itself was.

Ultimately, did he get quality care from people he felt like cared for him?

The HCAHPS QUESTION: Would you recommend this hospital to your friends and family?

Patients are just like you. They want family members and friends to have the best possible care. For a patient to be willing to recommend your hospital to a friend or family member, you need to provide the kind of care that you'd want your own mother or father or child to receive. It's an honor to have patients be willing to entrust the very life of someone they love to your hospital. It's important to work hard to be worthy of that honor.

...AND THE APPROACH AND TIPS THAT MAKE "10" AND "DEFINITELY YES" RESPONSES MORE LIKELY

These two questions are incredibly important. They are the culmination of every encounter patients have had with your hospital, from pre-admission to inpatient care to post-discharge follow-up. They are the "final grades" you get in the school of public (patient) opinion.

We are addressing them together in one chapter because they are highly correlated. In other words, if someone doesn't give your hospital a high rating on the 0 to 10 scale, he probably isn't going to recommend you to friends and family. In general, the things you do to get a favorable result on one question also lead to a favorable result on the other.

The three HCAHPS composites that are the most highly correlated statistically with these questions are nurse communication, pain management, and responsiveness of staff. So yes, you need to make absolutely certain your organization is well-versed in the tactics that impact these composites. (We'll discuss this a bit further shortly.)

But what really drives favorable results on these two HCAHPS questions is your culture. That's what patient responses really measure—your quality and your efficiency and effectiveness at delivering Individualized Patient Care. They answer the implied question: *Is everyone working to always provide this level of care to the patient?*

A Culture of *Always*

A culture of *always* is about taking your focus on providing excellent care from the bedside to the organization. It's about hardwiring excellence into your culture. Hardwiring is a measure of frequency. When you've hardwired something into every department, every process, and the mind of every staff member, that means "always."

A culture of *always* is also about making sure your Emergency Department—the major point of entry into your hospital—is the absolute best it can be. Remember, a bad ED experience is tough to overcome. And Studer Group research shows that as ED perception of care results improve, so do inpatient results.

When someone is willing to recommend your organization, that's about more than their clinical experience. It's about every person getting it right every time. Have you truly hardwired the kinds of behaviors that generate excellence—consistently?

In terms of HCAHPS, a culture of *always* means that everyone in the hospital is doing everything possible to make sure patients are so well served that they answer "always" to every appropriate survey question.

In larger, more holistic terms it means that everyone— from the CEO to the doctors to the nurses to the ancillary service and support service people—lives the hospital's mission to create the best place for patients to receive care...*always*. The entire organization holds themselves accountable to the standards of behavior that create the best environment and outcomes for the patient.

A culture of *always* has three major elements:

Alignment. This means all levels of your organization must have the same sense of urgency regarding HCAHPS and, in particular, its links to quality outcomes—not just senior leaders but all leaders and staff.

We recommend leaders at all levels regularly share the importance of HCAHPS and other issues regarding health reform with the people they supervise. They should connect the dots so that every staff member understands *why* these issues are important. Every employee needs to understand that executing the tactics that lead to great clinical quality (and, not incidentally, to high HCAHPS results) is critical to the hospital's financial future.

Consistency. A culture of *always* is synonymous with consistency. Every patient must have a consistently good experience no matter what department she's in, whether it's Monday morning or Saturday night, and no matter which leaders and staff members are working that day.

Of course, this is not an easy task to accomplish. It necessitates that proven best practices (many of which are included in this book) be hardwired into the organization. That begins with leadership. All leaders must speak in the same voice, follow the same processes and procedures, and work toward the same results. And all leaders and staff members need to understand why they're being asked to do what they're being asked to do—and to be held accountable for doing it.

Cross-organizational consistency leads to great clinical outcomes. It ensures that all patients and families have the best possible experience. It allows the hiring of the right employees and creates loyalty. It creates your organization's brand. And of course, it's good for your HCAHPS results.

Accountability. It's not enough to set performance goals. Hospitals must make sure people are actually achieving them. That may mean embracing new systems and processes that hold people at all levels accountable for executing well.

We have found that it's not unusual for healthcare organizations to overstate the performance of staff members. This may be due to poor evaluation tools. It's important that your evaluation tools are based on objective, measurable goals and that they allow you to weight certain areas higher than others for specific employees (to take into account various departmental goals).

Another common problem is an organization-wide failure to deal with low performers. (We've found that 40-60 percent of employees identified by their managers as "not meeting expectations" are not in any performance counseling.) Leaders must have a system for moving low performers up or out, improving the performance of middle performers, and re-recruiting high performers.

So, how do you achieve this level of alignment, consistency, and accountability...*always*? Simply, you make sure the right foundation is in place.

It All Comes Back to EBL

The one overarching approach that drives *always* is Evidence-Based Leadership[SM]. It is your framework to get to *always* and stay there. You might recall back in Chapter 1 that we mentioned Studer Group's Evidence-Based Leadership framework as a good foundation for moving HCAHPS results. We'd like to come back to this again.

Figure 17.1

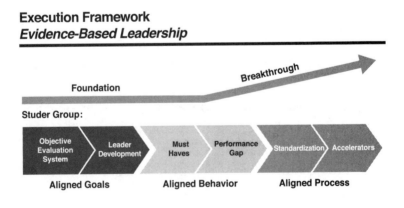

Execution Framework
Evidence-Based Leadership

If you have the EBL framework in place, you are well situated to create a culture of *always*. That's because all three major components of your organization—objective evaluation system, leadership development, and must-have behaviors—are aligned and work together in a cohesive, systematic way. And your processes are standardized and consistent, which allows people to execute effectively and opens the door to acceleration—the phase in which your outcomes start getting better and better.

When EBL is used systematically, the alignment creates a synergy that drives consistently excellent care to the patient—no matter where he is in the hospital and no matter which staff he is interacting with.

How Consistent Is Your Care?

Consistency is often where hospitals have the greatest opportunity for improvement. Some people may do certain things right all the time and some people may get it right some of the time but not all of the time. "Sometimes" is not good enough.

An inconsistent culture hurts you in many ways. It hinders your relationship with physicians, for instance. At Studer Group we hear about it all the time—physicians saying, "I want my patients on this unit, not that one," or, "Don't admit my patients on the weekend." Inconsistency also hurts your relationship with other staff members. For example, great nurses don't want to work with not-so-great nurses who don't seem to care. Organizational cultures in which this kind of inconsistency is allowed to exist can't provide the kind of care that leads to favorable HCAHPS responses.

Here's the bottom line: If we expect nurses to get to *always*, we need to expect *everyone* to get to *always*. Nurses can provide excellent care, but one negative interaction with someone else can cause a patient to be unwilling to recommend us and to not rank the hospital well.

We have found that when partners do well across the board, it's because they've moved from a culture of optionality to supporting tactics with a culture of *always*.

Of course, none of this is easy. Building a culture of *always* requires hard work from everyone, and results (whether they're in the form of higher HCAHPS performance or other quality metrics) won't come overnight. The good news is that as you're striving to transform your culture, there are certain things you can do to "jump start" your HCAHPS improvement.

Momentum Makers: Two Tips That Make a Big Difference

In this book we've given you plenty of tactics you can start implementing right away to improve your HCAHPS results in specific composites. And as we've discussed, they all work together with your culture to impact the two questions this chapter focuses on.

But perhaps you're looking for one or two changes you can make right now to accelerate your culture change and immediately impact the likelihood of patients giving you overall ratings of 9 or 10 and "definitely" being willing to recommend you. Here are two tips that give you plenty of bang for your buck:

Tip 1: Focus on Nursing Communication

Remember, the Nursing Communication composite is most highly correlated with both overall rating and willingness to recommend. That's why it makes sense to focus on it first. Best of all, when you improve nurse communication, your efforts will have a collateral effect on the other composites. For immediate impact:

- **Select units that provide the greatest opportunity for impact.** Focus on the units that have the highest number of discharges. These units will also have the highest number of surveys. Get it right here and you've already impacted a critical mass of patients.

   Then focus on the units that are performing at a mid-level (overall rank of 6, 7, or 8 and willingness to recommend of *probably yes*). Why? Just as it is easier to move a B grade to an A than a C grade to an A, it is easier to move middle results than poor results. Plus, getting a quick win here will boost the morale of everyone else.

- **Align nursing and ancillary goals.** Organizations tend to assume HCAHPS success rides on nursing, and much of it does. But as you may recall from the section on Nursing Communication, patients often think everyone who isn't a doctor is a nurse. That encompasses lots of staff members! We have found that other departments are the real key to getting from *usually* to *always* and *probably yes* to *definitely yes*.

As you focus on the Nurse Communication composite, remember those ancillary and support service teams that will partner with nurses to provide *always* care. For example, do the physical therapy leader and the nurse leader on Unit A both know that their goal is to bring up the results on the Nurse Communication composite? The physical therapy staff members who assist Unit A patients with ambulation can and do impact nursing communication. Aligned goals create a united front as both leaders work toward the same outcome.

Tip 2: Focus on the Emergency Department

Taking into account that an average of at least 50 percent of inpatients come in through the ED, and that results in the ED correlate to inpatient results, we advise you to recall what we said in Chapter 1: Don't underestimate the importance of the Emergency Department. We've found through intensive ED coaching that not only does providing an excellent experience in this critical department have an immediate impact on patient perception of inpatient care, it improves attending physician perception of quality and also improves ED throughput.

Here are three key tactics that support improvement in both the ED and inpatient experience:

- **Round first.** The first tactic to focus on in the ED is Rounding for Outcomes. It improves clinical outcomes, promotes safety, and increases efficiency. This tactic involves rounding on ED staff and patients much like we do in the inpatient setting. It also involves rounding in the reception area and at the bedside on an hourly basis. The goal is to manage pain, ensure that patients know their plans of care, and inform them of any potential delays. Rounding leads to more satisfied patients, staff, and physicians. It has also been proven to reduce patients leaving without treatment.

- **Implement bedside reporting.** This practice, which in best practice organizations is consistent with how it's done in the inpatient units, prevents medical errors and also builds employee teamwork, ownership, trust, and accountability. We recommend it be implemented only after hardwiring leader rounding on staff and patients to ensure there is a strong feedback loop for staff.

- **Conduct post-visit phone calls.** These calls improve clinical outcomes, increase patient satisfaction and market share, reduce formal complaints, help decrease costly and unnecessary readmissions, and save lives. In high-performing EDs, staff and physicians make calls daily with a goal to attempt to call 100 percent of eligible discharged patients and contact 60 percent of these patients within 72 hours after discharge. Organizations that use this best practice typically see results in 60 to 90 days, particularly in their ability to reduce readmissions.

The Time Is Now

Getting better and better is important for many reasons, health reform uppermost among them. As the rate of change in healthcare increases—due to pressure from the government, from insurers, from patients themselves—no hospital can afford to be standing still on the proverbial downward-moving escalator.

Make sure you're getting consistently positive results across *all* HCAHPS composites. (A high "willingness to recommend" coupled with lower numbers in other areas is a red flag.) Quickly and aggressively address variances in your results and commit yourself to steady improvement over time.

There's no doubt about it: HCAHPS is moving from a "pay-for-reporting" to a "pay-for-performance" initiative and is therefore an increasingly critical factor in your future. As more and more components of the Patient Protection and Affordable Care Act are phased in, hospitals that aren't constantly improving will see reimbursement decrease further and further. And because a hospital's financial health is inextricably linked to its ability to provide excellent care, constant upward trajectory in HCAHPS and other quality metrics doesn't just benefit you—it benefits your patients and your entire community.

Tools & Resources

Studer Group offers a variety of tools and resources that support the tactics discussed in this chapter. To access the most up-to-date offerings, please visit www.studergroup.com/HCAHPS.

To follow is a worksheet that will help you formulate a plan to improve patient perception of care regarding your overall rating and to increase the likelihood that patients will recommend your hospital.

Ultimately, healthcare organizations exist to serve humanity. The people drawn to this field are driven by a fierce desire to help others. By creating the kinds of organizations that patients sincerely rate "the best hospital possible"—the kind that they trust enough to recommend to the people they love—we are helping the men and women who work for us serve their highest sense of purpose. That is a true gift to all the healthcare professionals we work with, to the patients we serve, and to ourselves.

Even in those difficult circumstances when we cannot provide a cure or save a life, we know we can listen, be responsive, manage pain, and show compassion. In *Hardwiring Excellence*, Quint Studer writes that when his sister-in-law Kathy found out he was speaking at Advocate Christ Hospital in Oak Lawn, Illinois—the hospital to which she and her husband, Mike, were called on December 24, 1995, and informed that their 19-year-old son had died in a car accident—she asked him to convey a personal message. "Tell them thank you—they were so kind," Kathy requested of Quint.

It's times like these that illustrate what drives health-care professionals. Technology may be enhanced and payment systems may change—but what never changes is the dedication of these men and women to provide the very best care.

Overall Rating Planning Sheet

HCAHPS "TOP-BOX" PERCENTILES—December 2009 Public Reporting*

				Overall Rating Composite	
Percentile among reporting hospitals	5th	25th	50th	75th	95th
Percent of *always* responses	48	59	65	71	81

* These numbers are estimates based on historic national percentiles.

Current Overall Rating Result: _____

Converted to percentile: _____

90-Day Goal: _____ Percentile: _____

Action Plan:

Willingness to Recommend Planning Sheet

HCAHPS "TOP-BOX" PERCENTILES—December 2009 Public Reporting*

	Willingness to Recommend Composite				
Percentile among reporting hospitals	5th	25th	50th	75th	95th
Percent of *always* responses	50	61	68	74	85

* These numbers are estimates based on historic national percentiles.

Current Willingness to Recommend Result: _____

Converted to percentile: _____

90-Day Goal: _____ Percentile: _____

Action Plan:

CHAPTER EIGHTEEN:

THE IMPORTANCE OF VALIDATION: A CLOSING THOUGHT

Throughout this book we've talked about creating a culture of *always*. It's not enough to sometimes do the right thing. We must *always* do it—every department, every employee, every patient interaction. Otherwise, as we've discussed already, we may get the occasional spike in results, but we won't be able to consistently sustain a high level of performance—the level patients deserve.

As we at Studer Group® visit hospitals across the country, people sometimes tell us, "We cannot seem to get consistent results and hold them. We're doing Hourly Rounding℠. We're doing AIDET℠. But our HCAHPS results still aren't moving."

Our response is always: "But are you *really* doing them, fully focused on the outcomes, or are you just going through the motions? Are you doing them consistently? Are you doing them correctly? Are the tactics truly hardwired?"

If you hardwire the tactics we've covered in this book, and if you execute them as we've described them, you will see upward progress on your HCAHPS results. And best of all, you'll be able to maintain it over time.

If you're not seeing that upward progress—or if you're getting performance spikes that quickly subside—it's time to look at frequency, consistency, and quality. That's what validating is all about.

The process begins with diagnosis. Maybe overall you're strong in some composites and weak in others. Maybe certain departments are getting great results, and others are not. It sounds obvious but great outcomes start with knowing exactly where you need the most focus.

Make an effort to see the trees, not the forest. Really drill down, department by department, and analyze who is doing what well (and who isn't). Compare HCAHPS scores on composites across different departments. You may be able to harvest best practices within your organization and move them throughout the entire facility.

As you're doing this analysis, question everything. Is everyone truly aligned in their thinking about HCAHPS? Do all leaders and staff members have the skills they need? Have people been properly trained to implement the tactics? Are they being held accountable—*really* accountable—for doing so? Are their performance goals weighted to get them focused on the right things and to drive urgency?

You might discover that even though a tactic was officially "rolled out," it isn't being implemented with consistency. Maybe people were gung-ho on it for a little while, but then had an exceptionally busy week, stopped doing the tactic, and just never started back.

Maybe some people in your organization are doing the tactic all the time. Or maybe everyone's doing it some of the time.

Maybe people are *partially* implementing a tactic—doing some of the steps but missing other critical ones.

To some organizations, this kind of hit-or-miss approach is acceptable. We don't hold it up as the ideal, but we tolerate it—and remember, what we permit we promote.

Look at it this way: Few of us would ever compliment a doctor because he *usually* gets the pain medication right or *usually* performs the proper surgery or *usually* goes through all the steps in the surgery or *usually* visits his patients when he's on duty at the hospital. And very few doctors would ever accept that standard in themselves. So why should we let other staff members live in a "usually" world?

Usually isn't good enough for patients. They live in an "always" world. They expect us to *always* do what we should do to provide the best care for them. By focusing on HCAHPS and implementing the tactics in this book, we're creating the kind of environment they expect and deserve—an *always* environment.

You see the point: If everyone isn't consistently implementing the tactics they need to be implementing—and doing it correctly—HCAHPS results won't move. (Or, if they do, they won't move as quickly or as far as they should, and they certainly won't *stay* up.)

Once you've figured out that these tactics aren't really hardwired, you've won a big part of the battle. Then you can develop a game plan. For instance:

- Set up skills labs with senior leadership to ensure their individual leaders are meeting frequency and quality standards.
- Implement a process improvement initiative. Often, it's ineffective or broken processes that create barriers to success. Remember, outcomes are dependent upon two things: processes and people. If there's a lack of process structure or inconsistency in how people are carrying out the behaviors, variances will occur and the *always* factor will be minimized.
- Perform audit rounds by unit to make sure tactics like Hourly Rounding and AIDET are being done properly.
- Do HCAHPS training. (Make sure every employee is able to state his or her role in HCAHPS.)

Some leaders worry that validating seems like "checking up" on people—as if the implication is that we don't trust them. But validation isn't a matter of trust. It's a matter of process and a matter of quality. It's making sure that we're not just going through the motions but are truly performing tactics in a way that gets results. And it's applying the key learnings that result to your future process efforts.

Most people in healthcare want to do their best possible work. They appreciate it when leaders help them improve. Not only does validating achieve that goal, it's a good way of rewarding and recognizing high performers. It's a way of ensuring that the departments driving your HCAHPS results set a performance standard for the rest of the organization.

Validation is a critical part of creating a culture of *always*.

In the end, validating leads to better outcomes. In fact, when you really connect the dots, you'll see that it saves lives. Isn't that why we're all here?

Acknowledgments

So many different people have left their fingerprints on this book. Without the experience and the insights of countless industry professionals, both inside and outside Studer Group®, *The HCAHPS Handbook* could never have come to be. To all of them, we offer a collective and heartfelt thank you.

Specifically, we would like to extend our gratitude to:

The leaders of Studer Group partner organizations across the nation...

Thank you for your commitment to using Evidence-Based Leadership℠ to create a culture of *always*, so your patients consistently get the best care. By sharing your results and best practices with Studer Group, you've enabled us to build a national learning lab of hundreds and hundreds of hospitals. Thanks to this coalition of top industry minds, we can all learn from each other.

Thank you specifically to the partners below for providing assistance to material in these pages.

- Kaiser Permanente, Portland, OR
- North Austin Medical Center, Austin, TX
- St. Alexius Medical Center, Hoffman Estates, IL
- Beaver Dam Community Hospitals, Beaver Dam, WI
- Palmetto Baptist Easley, Easley, SC
- Homestead Hospital, Homestead, FL

The Studer Group experts who coach these organizations...

Your tireless work on the frontlines is making a difference in hospitals and organizations everywhere.

An extra helping of gratitude goes to those coaches who directly provided their insight and expertise during the writing of *The HCAHPS Handbook*:

- Judy Kees
- Terry Rose
- Lyn Ketelsen
- Tonia Breckenridge
- Julie Kennedy-Oehlert

...And the other individuals who made it all come together.

We deeply appreciate your dedication, which sometimes took the form of weekends and late-night hours spent reviewing manuscripts and sharing the insight and expertise you've gained from your travels throughout the country. Many thanks to:

Stephen Beeson, MD—Your contributions on the subjects of doctor communication and explanation of medications were immensely helpful to us as we wrote *The HCAHPS Handbook*. We gleaned lots of information from your books, *Practicing Excellence* and *Engaging Physicians*, and we hope that readers will reference both to learn more.

Barbara Loeb, MD—Thank you for sharing your work and your insights on what matters to physicians, the impact HCAHPS will have on them, and the art of building nurse/physician relationships.

Davy Crockett—We appreciate your early input and the hours you spent combing through partner research to ensure that the best and most effective tactics were highlighted in the book.

Faye Sullivan—Your initial review of materials really helped move the content of this book up a notch.

Stephanie Baker—Thank you for your final review of the book (done the moment you returned from vacation!), the wisdom that comes from all your hard work, and especially your Emergency Department expertise. Your book, *Excellence in the Emergency Department*, proved to be a rich resource for us.

Dottie DeHart and team—Thank you for taking the down-and-dirty tactics and content provided by three very different personalities and turning them into a cohesive, didactic tool. You did a fabulous job, as always, and we appreciate your talent and professionalism.

Last but not least, Bekki Kennedy—The hours you spent researching mountains of material and distilling it down to the "best of the best" built the foundation for this book. Thank you for bringing structure to *The HCAHPS Handbook* and coordinating countless versions of chapters in various stages of editing as they moved back and forth between authors and reviewers.

If we've left anyone out of this list, we offer our deepest apologies. A book like this is truly magical. It's tangible evidence that human beings can come together and create something greater than the sum of its parts—something that changes the way hospitals operate, touches the lives of patients, and leaves the world a bit better off than it was before.

RESOURCES

Accelerate the momentum of your Healthcare Flywheel®.
Access additional resources at www.studergroup.com/HCAHPS.

STUDER GROUP COACHING:

Studer Group® coaches hospitals and healthcare systems providing detailed framework and practical how-tos that create change. Studer Group coaches work side-by-side establishing, accelerating, and hardwiring the necessary changes to create a culture of excellence. In our work, Studer Group has identified a core of three critical elements that must be in place for great organizational performance once a commitment is made to the pillar approach to goal setting and the Nine Principles® of Behavior.

Emergency Department Coaching Line

Is a comprehensive approach to improving service and operational efficiency in the Emergency Department. Our team of ED coach experts will partner with you to implement best practices, proven tools, and tactics using our Evidence-Based Leadership^{SM} approach to improve results in all five pillars—People, Service, Quality, Finance, and Growth. Key deliverables include decreasing staff turnover, improving employee, physician, and patient satisfaction, decreasing door-to-doctor times, reducing left without being seen rates, increasing upfront cash collections, and increasing patient volumes and revenue.

To learn more about Studer Group coaching, visit www.studergroup.com.

BOOKS: categorized by audience

Senior Leaders & Physicians

Leadership and Medicine—A book that makes sense of the complex challenges of healthcare and offers a wealth of practical advice to future generations, written by Floyd D. Loop, MD, former chief executive of the Cleveland Clinic (1989-2004).

Engaging Physicians: A Manual to Physician Partnership—A tactical and passionate roadmap for physician collaboration to generate organizational high performance, written by Stephen C. Beeson, MD.

Straight A Leadership: Alignment, Action, Accountability—A guide that will help you identify gaps in
Alignment, Action, and Accountability, create a plan to
fill them, and become a more resourceful, agile, high-
performing organization, written by Quint Studer.

Excellence with an Edge: Practicing Medicine in a
Competitive Environment—An insightful book that provides practical tools and techniques you need to know to
have a solid grasp of the business side of making a living
in healthcare, written by Michael T. Harris, MD.

Physicians

Practicing Excellence: A Physician's Manual to Exceptional Health Care—This book, written by Stephen C.
Beeson, MD, is a brilliant guide to implementing physician leadership and behaviors that will create a high-
performance workplace.

All Leaders

Hardwiring Excellence—A *BusinessWeek* bestseller, this
book is a road map to creating and sustaining a "Culture of Service and Operational Excellence" that drives
bottom-line results.
Written by Quint Studer

Results That Last—A *Wall Street Journal* bestseller by
Quint Studer that teaches leaders in every industry how
to apply his tactics and strategies to their own organizations to build a corporate culture that consistently
reaches and exceeds its goals.

Hardwiring Flow: Systems and Processes for Seamless Patient Care—Drs. Thom Mayer and Kirk Jensen delve into one of the most critical issues facing healthcare leaders today: patient flow.

Eat That Cookie!: Make Workplace Positivity Pay Off... For Individuals, Teams, and Organizations—Written by Liz Jazwiec, RN, this book is funny, inspiring, relatable, and is packed with realistic, down-to-earth tactics to infuse positivity into your culture.

"I'm Sorry to Hear That..." Real Life Responses to Patients' 101 Most Common Complaints About Health Care—When you respond to a patient's complaint, you are responding to the patient's sense of helplessness and anxiety. The service recovery scripts offered in this book can help you recover a patient's confidence in you and your organization. Authored by Susan Keane Baker and Leslie Bank.

What's Right in Health Care: 365 Stories of Purpose, Worthwhile Work, and Making a Difference—A collaborative effort of stories from healthcare professionals across the nation. This 742-page book shares a story a day submitted by your friends and colleagues. It is a daily reminder about why we answered this calling and why we stay with it—to serve a purpose, to do worthwhile work, and to make a difference.

101 Answers to Questions Leaders Ask—By Quint Studer and Studer Group coaches, offers practical, pre-

scriptive solutions to some of the many questions he's received from healthcare leaders around the country.

Nurse Leaders and Nurses
The Nurse Leader Handbook: The Art and Science of Nurse Leadership—By Studer Group senior nursing and physician leaders from across the country, is filled with knowledge that provides nurse leaders with a solid foundation for success. It also serves as a reference they can revisit again and again when they have questions or need a quick refresher course in a particular area of the job.

Inspired Nurse and Inspired Journal—By Rich Bluni, RN, helps maintain and recapture the inspiration nurses felt at the start of their journey with action-oriented "spiritual stretches" and stories that illuminate those sacred moments we all experience.

Emergency Department Team
Excellence in the Emergency Department—A book by Stephanie Baker, RN, CEN, MBA, is filled with proven, easy-to-implement, step-by-step instructions that will help you move your Emergency Department forward.

For more information about books and other resources, visit www.firestarterpublishing.com.

MAGAZINES:

Hardwired Results - Issue 11, 2009
Tools to create accountability and add dollars to your bottom line

Hardwired Results - Issue 12, 2009
Offers a wealth of evidence-backed insights on addressing the three "As"—Alignment, Action, Accountability—to achieve peak performance.

Visit www.studergroup.com to view additional *Hardwired Results* magazines.

ARTICLES:

Keep Your Patients Coming Back
MGMA Connexion
August 2008

Quint Studer on 5 Important Issues Facing Healthcare Leaders
The Hospital Review
November 14, 2008

Unlocking the FEAR Foothold
Quint Studer
March 2009

Evidence-Based Leadership
Projects@Work
Quint Studer

How to Achieve and Sustain Excellence
Healthcare Financial Management

To read these articles and view other resources, please visit www.studergroup.com.

SOFTWARE SOLUTIONS:

Leader Evaluation Manager™: Results Through Focus and Accountability

Studer Group's Leader Evaluation Manager is a web-based application that automates the goal setting and performance review process for all leaders, while ensuring that the performance metrics of individual leaders are aligned with the overall goals of the organization. By using Leader Evaluation Manager, both leaders and their supervisors will clearly understand from the beginning of the year what goals need to be accomplished to achieve a successful annual review, can plan quarterly tasks with completion targets under each goal, and view monthly report cards to manage progress.

To learn more, please visit www.firestarterpublishing.com.

INSTITUTES:

Taking You and Your Organization to the Next Level with Quint Studer

Learn the tools, tactics, and strategies that are needed to Take You and Your Organization to the Next Level at this two-day institute with Quint Studer and Studer Group's Coach Experts. You will walk away with your passion ignited, and with Evidence-Based Leadership^{SM} strategies to create a sustainable culture of excellence.

Nuts and Bolts of Operational Excellence in the Emergency Department

Improve patient flow and build service and operational excellence in your Emergency Department as Jay Kaplan, MD, FACEP, and Stephanie Baker, RN, CEN, MBA, both with extensive and ongoing real-life ED experience, share proven tactics such as Provider in Triage, Rounding for Outcomes, Discharge Phone Calls, Key Words at Key Times, and AIDET^{SM}.

What's Right in Health Care^{SM}

One of the largest healthcare peer-to-peer learning conferences in the nation, *What's Right in Health Care* brings organizations together to share ideas that have been proven to make healthcare better.

To review a listing of Studer Group institutes or to register for an institute, visit www.studergroup.com/institutes.

For information on Continuing Education Credits, visit www.studergroup.com/cmecredits.

Visit www.studergroup.com/HCAHPS to access and download many of the resources, examples, and tools mentioned in *The HCAHPS Handbook*.

QUINT STUDER

Quint Studer is founder and CEO of Studer Group®, an outcomes firm that implements Evidence-Based Leadership^SM systems and practices that help organizations thrive in times of change by attaining and sustaining outstanding results. He spends much of his time creating, harvesting, and sharing best practices from his company's "national learning lab" of hundreds of organizations and thousands of leaders.

Inc. magazine named Studer its Master of Business, making him the only healthcare leader to have ever won this award. Twice *Modern Healthcare* has chosen him as one of the 100 Most Powerful People in Healthcare.

Studer's most recent book, *Straight A Leadership*, teaches senior leaders how to create organizations that can execute swiftly and well in response to a rapidly shifting external environment. He has also written two bestselling titles. His first, *Business Week* bestseller *Hardwiring Excellence*, is one of the bestselling leadership books ever written for healthcare. More than 350,000 copies have been sold. His second book, *Results That Last*, hit the *Wall Street Journal's* bestseller list of business books.

BRIAN C. ROBINSON

Brian C. Robinson is executive vice president at Studer Group. He serves as an advisor on health policy and industry affairs for the outcomes firm. Brian conceptualized Studer Group's patient call manager, *The Clinical Call System*™, a fully HIPAA-compliant web-hosted system that automates the process of making pre-visit and post-discharge calls and provides documentation for the medical record.

Before joining Studer Group, Brian was a CEO for 20 years. He has led small rural hospitals, large urban teaching facilities, and most recently Las Vegas's busiest system of hospitals and clinics. Under his leadership, his facilities have had the distinction of being named in America's "Top 100 Hospitals" eight times.

Brian has often been called upon for his expertise in Washington, D.C., where he has been appointed by the Secretary of Health and Human Services to serve as a technical advisor to CMS. He has served as a member, board of directors, of the Federation of American Hospitals and has served as chair, CEO committee, Federation of American Hospitals.

He earned his bachelor's degree in business administration and biology from Phillips University and a master's degree in health services administration from Arizona State University.

Brian speaks nationally on health reform, HCAHPS, and other key industry issues.

KAREN COOK, RN

Karen Cook, RN, has been a registered nurse for more than 30 years and a senior coach with Studer Group for more than a decade. She has coached leaders at some of the largest healthcare systems in the United States.

Since 2005 Karen has coached hospitals participating in the HCAHPS survey process, including participating in early focus groups with the Agency for Healthcare Research and Quality. She was the primary author of one of the industry's first HCAHPS toolkits. This resource, published by Studer Group in 2007, became a springboard for *The HCAHPS Handbook*.

The Studer Group partners she works with have received numerous awards and accolades including Magnet facility, Top 50 Hospitals, and Top 100 Places to Work designations. They've also earned patient satisfaction achievements like Client Success Story and the Summit Award.

Karen is a national speaker known for her passionate, enthusiastic style and her ability to "get to the heart of the matter."

How to Order Additional Copies of

The HCAHPS Handbook
Hardwire Your Hospital for
Pay-for-Performance Success

Orders may be placed:

Online at:
www.firestarterpublishing.com
www.studergroup.com

By phone at: 866-354-3473

By mail at: Fire Starter Publishing
913 Gulf Breeze Parkway, Suite 6
Gulf Breeze, FL 32561

(Bulk discounts are available.)

The HCAHPS Handbook
is also available online at www.amazon.com.